CAMBRIDGE
UNIVERSITY PRESS

Cambridge Lower Secondary
English
LEARNER'S BOOK 8

Graham Elsdon

CAMBRIDGE
UNIVERSITY PRESS

University Printing House, Cambridge CB2 8BS, United Kingdom

One Liberty Plaza, 20th Floor, New York, NY 10006, USA

477 Williamstown Road, Port Melbourne, VIC 3207, Australia

314–321, 3rd Floor, Plot 3, Splendor Forum, Jasola District Centre, New Delhi – 110025, India

79 Anson Road, #06–04/06, Singapore 079906

Cambridge University Press is part of the University of Cambridge.

It furthers the University's mission by disseminating knowledge in the pursuit of education, learning and research at the highest international levels of excellence.

www.cambridge.org
Information on this title: www.cambridge.org/9781108746632

First published 2012
Second edition 2021

20 19 18 17 16 15 14 13 12 11 10 9 8 7 6 5 4 3 2 1

Printed in Malaysia by Vivar Printing

A catalogue record for this publication is available from the British Library

ISBN 978-1-108-74663-2 Paperback with Digital Access (1 Year)
ISBN 978-1-108-74664-9 Digital Learner's Book (1 Year)
ISBN 978-1-108-74660-1 eBook

Cambridge University Press has no responsibility for the persistence or accuracy of URLs for external or third-party internet websites referred to in this publication, and does not guarantee that any content on such websites is, or will remain, accurate or appropriate. Information regarding prices, travel timetables, and other factual information given in this work is correct at the time of first printing but Cambridge University Press does not guarantee the accuracy of such information thereafter.

....

....

Third-party websites, publications and resources referred to in this publication have not been endorsed by Cambridge Assessment International Education.

〉Introduction

Welcome to Stage 8 of Cambridge Lower Secondary English.

We have designed this book not only to help you extend your English skills, but also to introduce you to some fantastic stories and articles from around the world.

You will encounter dramatic tales about dangerous animals, mysterious islands and deadly situations. You will also discuss important topics, such as climate change and how humans treat nature. There is a wide range of fiction and non-fiction texts from international writers, all of which have been specially chosen to appeal to readers of your age.

You will read two full-length stories in this book. The first one, 'Grandmother's Song', explores the importance of families and growing up. The second, 'The Plantation', is about a discovery that leads to disastrous consequences. Both stories will give you a good understanding of how writers structure their work, and allow you to explore themes in a more detailed way.

We hope you will enjoy writing stories in a variety of genres, such as fantasy and adventure, as well as practising your argumentative skills. There are opportunities to study poetry, perform your own drama script, and use language in lively, interesting ways.

You will also have many opportunities for speaking and listening as you discuss your responses to texts and issues affecting your lives. The projects at the end of each unit build on the knowledge you have acquired, and allow you to practise the key skills of research and presentation that you will need for future study and work.

We really want you to enjoy the texts and activities in this book, and make use of the assessment and reflection features. They will help develop your independent learning skills, and will allow you to see just how much progress you are making.

Good luck on the next stage of your learning journey.

Graham Elsdon

Contents

	Writing	Speaking/Listening	Language focus	21st century skills
	Audio drama; writing informally; imaginative accounts	Pair discussion and prediction; script reading; discussing views; audio biography; reading a poem aloud; discussing text structure	Verb tenses for effect; features of poetry: end-stopping/ enjambment/caesura; formal and informal language; strategies for working out unfamiliar words	Creativity; collaboration
	Combining techniques; analysis of structure; writing dialogue; analysing theme; biographical account	Pair and group discussion; unseen dialogue	Figurative language; reporting verbs to show character and mood	Critical thinking; communication
	Writing a monologue; writing a play; account from a character's viewpoint	Pair discussion; individual speaking; performing a play	Punctuation for effect; dialogue in play scripts; strategies for spelling unfamiliar words	Collaboration; creativity
	An article for an older audience; a persuasive speech; a story submission; describing setting	Pair and group discussion	Placement of sentence types for effect; clarity of language; choice of synonyms	Creativity; critical thinking
	Writing a counter-argument; a character in a challenging setting; a blog from a character's point of view; film script	Pair discussion; script performance; debating views	Coordinating conjunctions and subordinating conjunctions in argument writing; imperatives and modal verbs in advice texts	Social responsibility; collaboration
	Account writing; design a leaflet; write a fable; comparing poems; imaginative account	Pair and group discussion	Emotive language; extended metaphors	Critical thinking; learning to learn
	Diary entries; understanding characters; monologues; analysing technique combination; personal account from character's perspective; report writing	Pair and group discussion; monologue; news report	Adjectives to show specific qualities; active and passive voice	Social responsibility; creativity
	Writing a drama scene; writing a poem; account writing; personal response; writing an argument	Pair, group reading/ performance and individual discussion	Adverbs of manner and degree; adverbs of time; linking adverbs; prepositional phrases	Learning to learn; communication
	Responding to feelings; comparing poems; trailer script writing; debating heroism	Pair, group and individual discussion	Coordinating conjunctions; present participles	Creativity; collaboration

> How to use this book

This book contains lots of different features that will help your learning. These are explained below.

This list sets out what you will learn in each session. You can use these points to identify the important topics for the lesson.

> **In this session, you will:**
> - perform a section of dialogue from a story
> - write an audioscript based on a prose text
> - work out the meaning of unfamiliar words
> - give a reasoned response to a text using references.

This contains questions or activities to help find out what you know already about the topics in this session.

> **Getting started**
>
> How would you define the word 'verb'? In pairs, write a list of verb types with examples. Then think of a wild animal and describe how it moves to your partner, using powerful verbs. For example, 'This animal sprints across grassland, hunting its antelope prey' (a cheetah). Try to guess each other's animal.

Important words are highlighted in the text when they first appear in the book. You will find an explanation of the meaning of these words in the margin. You will also find definitions of all these words in the glossary at the back of this book.

> **Key words**
>
> fiction: stories about imaginary characters and events
>
> tone: the way that someone speaks or how a piece of writing sounds, which helps suggest mood and feelings

Activities give you the opportunity to practise and develop the skills that you learn in each session. Activities will involve answering questions or completing tasks. This includes listening activities where you hear a sound recording. These recordings can be played from the Digital edition of the Learner's Book. Your Digital edition also includes recordings of all the text extracts.

> 08　1　Tu Fu was a Chinese poet who lived more than 2500 years ago. Listen to the podcast about Tu Fu. As you listen, make notes about the poet's life.
>
> Divide your notes into main points, covering the significant dates and events in his life, and subsidiary points (minor details about his life). Use any method you prefer to make these notes, such as bullet points, a spider diagram or a table.

This will provide you with explanations of important content relating to grammar and language.

> **Language focus**
>
> In poetry, different effects can be created by varying the length of lines and how they are punctuated.
> - Some lines of poetry have a punctuation mark at the end – they are **end-stopped** or use a comma.
> - Sometimes a poet will use **enjambment** to create a sense of movement or to make the poem sound like a monologue.
> - Poets may also decide to use punctuation in the middle of a line (**caesura**) to signify a pause.

Each tip will help you to develop a technique or skill connected to reading, writing, speaking or listening.

> **Speaking tip**
>
> When reading dialogue aloud, remember to think about the **context**. Consider who your character is speaking to, how they might be feeling and any actions they would be carrying out at that point in the story.

After completing an activity, this provides you with the opportunity to either assess your own work or another learner's work.

This contains questions that ask you to look back at what you have covered and reflect on your learning.

- What were the challenges of comparing two poems?
- What advice would you give to someone about to attempt this activity?

This list summarises the important skills that you have learnt in the session.

Summary checklist

☐ I can use a variety of strategies effectively to work out the meaning of unfamiliar words.

☐ I can use precise vocabulary to describe feelings and emotions related to events.

These questions look back at some of the content you learnt in each session in this unit. If you can answer these, you are ready to move on to the next unit.

Check your progress

Answer these questions.

1 What is the difference in effect between a present tense verb and past tense verb? Give some examples.
2 Describe the main differences between a drama script and prose writing.
3 Give some examples of figurative language.
4 Explain the impact of the placement of punctuation choices in poems – what effect is created by end-stopping, enjambment and caesura?
5 Give an example of a compound-complex sentence.
6 Explain two strategies for working out the meaning of unfamiliar words.

At the end of each unit, there is a group project that you can carry out with other learners. This will involve using some of the knowledge that you learnt during the unit. Your project might involve creating or producing something, or you might all solve a problem together.

Project

Who would you include in a list of modern real-life heroes? In this project, you are going to work in a group and give a talk about a hero.

An international company wants to make a series of short films about modern heroes. The film series will be called *My 21st Century Hero*. They want young people to talk about somebody they admire – a figure from a sporting, musical, creative, scientific or environmental background. They must have been alive in the 21st century.

As a group, your task is to persuade the international company to make a film about your chosen hero. Start by discussing and researching possible heroes that you could talk about, after which you must agree on *one* hero to present. Once you have done this, prepare your talk.

Each person in the group must say something about the hero, including their background, what they have achieved and why they are admired. Most importantly, you need to persuade the company why they should make a film about your hero.

The talk should last five minutes.

Nature and humans

In this unit, you will explore the ways that people interact with nature. You will read extracts from a novel, analyse a series of poems and consider environmental issues. As you work through the texts and activities, think about how they show the relationship between people and nature.

> 1.1 The leopard

In this session, you will:

- look at how structural features can be used for effect

- consider how verbs can be used in descriptions

- explore how a writer combines structural and language techniques

- discuss what might happen next in a story.

Getting started

How would you define the word 'verb'? In pairs, write a list of verb types with examples. Then think of a wild animal and describe how it moves to your partner, using powerful verbs. For example, 'This animal sprints across grassland, hunting its antelope prey' (a cheetah). Try to guess each other's animal.

When the Mountains Roared

This extract is from a novel called *When the Mountains Roared* by Jess Butterworth. It tells the story of Ruby, a girl living in India. In this passage, she is walking in the mountains, taking pictures with her friend Praveen. They encounter two people who they recognise, Toad and Stinger, with another man.

Extract 1

The tallest mountain peaks are always there in the distance. The sun rises behind them. At dawn the air fills with birds and tweets. In the growing light, Praveen spots the remains of a camp fire at the side of the path. We run and place our hands over it. It's still warm.

We walk higher and higher, climbing up to the clouds.

'My mum always says that up in the mountains there are fewer people, which means there are fewer thoughts. It's one of the reasons it's so peaceful,' says Praveen.

I'd never thought about it like that before. The air is thinner up here. I can feel it in my chest. I hear twigs cracking up ahead.

Praveen raises his finger to his lips. We tiptoe onwards. A smaller path has been made through the trees, off the main path.

Praveen beckons me that way. I grip the camera in my hand.

Suddenly, a shot rings out into the air. It echoes off the mountains, disturbing the stillness.

I duck behind some ferns, pulling Praveen down with me. We crawl forwards on our hands and knees towards the sound. I can hear men's voices ahead. Peering between ferns, I see Toad and Stinger, and a tall man who must be the film star, Garjan Mankar.

In front of them is a leopard.

1   Read Extract 1 again. As you read, make notes on:

a   the impression of nature the writer gives in the first three paragraphs

b   which characters seem 'good' and which 'bad'.

2   In **fiction**, writers structure their stories to include and develop different **tones** and effects. In this extract, the writer initially establishes a peaceful tone, but as the story develops a sense of danger emerges.

In pairs, carry out the following tasks:

a   **Summarise** the story so far.

b   Identify the point in the extract where the tone changes.

c   Make notes on the effect this change of tone has on the reader.

Key words

fiction: stories about imaginary characters and events

tone: the way that someone speaks or how a piece of writing sounds, which helps suggest mood and feelings

summarise: to explain the main points of a text in a few words

Language focus

When selected carefully, verbs can really bring a description to life. One of the key decisions writers make is which verb tense to use. Past tense verbs describe events that have already happened. The difference in time between when the story is narrated and when it occurred adds some distance to the tale. This can make a story seem more natural – when we recount experiences, we do so from a point *after* they have occurred. Present tense verbs make the action seem more immediate, which can create a sense of excitement, drawing the reader into the story. Look at these examples.

• Amir blasted the football over the wall.

The past tense verb has the effect of looking back at a dramatic moment. The action seems to 'stand still' as we observe Amir's actions at a distance from a point in the future.

• Amir blasts the football over the wall.

Here the actions seems immediate, almost as if we are there at the moment it takes place.

3   In Extract 1, the writer uses present tense verbs such as *rises*, *spots* and *walk*. Write a paragraph commenting on the verbs the writer has chosen to build detail in this extract. You should also explain the effect of using the present tense.

One of the **themes** of this story is how human actions can harm nature. In Extract 2, Ruby and Praveen see what the men do to the leopard. The writer combines language, **characterisation** and **structural features** to heighten the effect of sadness and cruelty at what happens. Think about this as you read the extract.

Extract 2

The leopard knows it's cornered and faces them snarling. Its body is low to the ground.

'Run,' I whisper under my breath. 'Why don't you run?'

But then I notice one of its back paws is stained with blood. It can only limp.

My heart leaps; it must be the same leopard I saw before.

She growls, warning them not to come closer.

It happens so fast. A click, and then the crack of their guns.

'No!' I scream.

My voice is lost beneath the sound of shooting.

And it's too late. There's nothing I can do. The beautiful leopard thuds to the ground. I collapse against a tree. And the mountains roar with me.

*

The leopard lies on its stomach; a sandy-coloured coat covered in black rosettes. Its front legs are spread in front of it, with its long white tail curled round its side. The coat has a velvet sheen all over except for the bullet wound in its side.

The men tower over it, clasping their rifles. Stinger kneels, touching the leopard's fur.

'It's not a snow leopard, but it has one beautiful coat,' says Garjan admiringly. He removes his sunglasses and rests them on top of his head.

Evidence. This leopard's death can't be in vain. With shaky hands I grip the camera and switch it on. It whirs as the lens pushes out. I raise it up and focus through the leaves.

> 'Wait, Ruby,' whispers Praveen behind me. 'Wait—'
>
> I press the shutter.
>
> Click.
>
> The air around me is bathed in bright white light as the camera flashes.
>
> The men look up in our direction, dazed for a split second.
>
> I forgot about the flash.

4   Look at this list of features of characterisation, structure and language in the story. Write a brief explanation for each one, commenting on its effect and using an example from the text.

- the leopard is seen as a victim **figure**

- the men are seen as villain figures

- the link between the **narrator** and the leopard

- vocabulary to show the beauty of the leopard

- powerful verbs showing what happens to the leopard and how the narrator reacts.

Key words

figure: a recognisable type of character in a story, such as a hero, villain, victim

narrator: the person telling the story

Reading tip

When analysing a writer's methods, remember that the most important aspect is the effect that particular methods and techniques have on the reader. Briefly identify the techniques, then focus your comments on their effect.

- In Activity 4, did you find it easier to write about features such as characterisation (the first two bullet points), structure (the third bullet) or language features (the last two bullet points)?

- Why do you think that is?

- How could you improve your skills at writing about these methods and techniques?

5 Extract 2 ends with a real sense of danger. In pairs, discuss what you think will happen next. Share your ideas about what you would do next if you were Ruby.

Summary checklist

☐ I understand how a writer structures a story to create specific effects.

☐ I can explain how verbs can be used to bring descriptions to life.

☐ I can analyse the effect of language and structural choices in a text.

☐ I can develop a discussion, sharing and listening to ideas on what might happen next in a story.

› 1.2 The mysterious figure

In this session, you will:

- perform a section of dialogue from a story
- write an audioscript based on a prose text
- work out the meaning of unfamiliar words
- give a reasoned response to a text using references.

Getting started

What are the main differences between stories written in **prose** and those written as drama **scripts**? In pairs, make a list of the features of both types of writing and compare them.

Key words

prose: the form of language found in novels and non-fiction texts such as articles, written in paragraphs rather than verse

script: the words and actions from a play written down for the actors to use

Read the next part of *When the Mountains Roared.*

Extract 3

'Get back,' I say to Praveen.

Toad reacts first. He bellows and charges towards us.

In an instant, strong hands clasp around my arms, yanking me up. He tugs the camera from around my neck, breaking the strap, and hurls it against a rock. It smashes into pieces.

'No,' I say, rushing towards it. 'All my photos are stored on there.'

Stinger heaves Praveen from the undergrowth.

'What are you doing out here?' Toad barks.

'Who are you working for?' yells Garjan, his gaze wild. 'Are you taking pictures of me?'

'We were taking pictures of animals,' I say, quickly. 'I'm practising to be a wildlife photographer.'

I can't stop looking at the dead leopard. I wonder if it's the same one I met eyes with, that day in the jungle. The one that watched me. The one I vowed to protect. I shake Stinger off and kneel next to it, touching the soft fur, to make sure. There's no heartbeat.

'You killed it,' I hiss at the film star. 'You coward.'

His handsome face flushes red.

'I've had enough of this,' says Toad, grabbing Praveen's arms and forcing them behind his back. 'Get her!'

Stinger's hands close around my wrists.

A silhouette appears on the ridge above us.

1 This part of the story is very dramatic. It shows characters in conflict, experiencing a range of emotions. It includes **dialogue** and ends on a moment of tension – the reader is unsure whose side the unnamed person is on.

In groups of three, read the dialogue – the words spoken by the narrator (Ruby), Toad and Garjan. Use your voice and **gestures** to show the emotions they are feeling.

Speaking tip

When reading dialogue aloud, remember to think about the **context**. Consider who your character is speaking to, how they might be feeling and any actions they would be carrying out at that point in the story.

2 In groups of three, rewrite Extract 3 as an **audio drama** script. Use the original dialogue but remember that drama scripts do not have a narrator, so you will need to consider how to convey the information that comes from the description rather than the dialogue. You will need to show the confrontation, the narrator's thoughts about the leopard and the shadowy figure that appears at the end. You could do this by adding more dialogue or using sound effects.

Remember to add names into the dialogue so listeners will know who the characters are talking to. For example, **RUBY:** *Get back, Praveen!* tells the reader who Ruby is talking to.

Peer assessment

Swap scripts with another group.

- What details did the other group include in the script that were not in yours?
- Were these details important or effective?
- How well do you think a listening audience would be able to follow the action from the script? Give feedback, explaining your reasons.

Key words

dialogue: conversation between two or more characters, written as direct speech

gesture: movements of the hands or arms to add emphasis or bring a story to life

context: the situation within which something exists or happens

audio drama: a play that is heard, rather than seen, by the audience

stage directions: words in a script that explain what is happening on stage or tell the actors how to move and speak

Writing tip

Scripts are set out in specific ways. Character names are written at the side and tone of voice is shown in brackets. Sound effects and **stage directions** are also shown in the body of the script.

Now read the next part of the story.

Extract 4

Grandma stands over us all.

'Let them go,' she calls. Her voice is calm, icy. It sends shivers down my spine.

There's a stunned silence, and then Toad laughs.

'I'm giving you one more chance. Get away from them or I'll shoot,' she says again.

'Go and get her too,' says Toad to Stinger.

Stinger hesitates, then takes a step forward.

A bullet skims the branches above us. I can feel it whistling through the air.

'Next time I shoot, I'll be aiming for you,' Grandma says.

'Let them go,' says Garjan, stumbling backwards.

'But …' says Toad.

'Do what the old lady wants,' he shouts, brushing off his leather jacket.

While they're distracted, I scramble along the dirt for the camera. The blue memory card is on the ground, half-hidden under some leaves. I grab it. It's cracked down the middle. I shove it quickly into my pocket.

I bend down and <u>rummage</u> through the branches. Something scratches my wrist. I yank my hand back.

'Ouch,' I say. Then I see movement and a blur of spots. I part the <u>foliage</u>, more carefully this time. Two wide eyes stare back at me. A cub, falling over its hind legs as it tries to back away.

I reach forward and grab its soft warm fur.

It opens its mouth and gives a tiny roar. A high-pitched, scratchy sound.

It's calling for its mother.

> 'Is that a cub?' asks Praveen, in awe.
>
> I nod and hide the leopard cub in the inside of my jacket to keep it calm and carry it down the slope. As I <u>cradle</u> the cub, my heart feels ready to burst with love for it.
>
> The mountain is silent apart from howling wind.

3   One way to work out the meanings of words that are unfamiliar to you is to look at their context. This means reading the words around the unfamiliar word and understanding what is happening in the story at that point.

For example, look at the word *rummage* in the extract. Now look carefully at the whole sentence, and at what happens just before and just after it. You know that the narrator is looking for the memory card among the branches so you can make a sensible guess that *rummage* means 'to search roughly'. Work out what the words *foliage* and *cradle* mean. Then check your answers in a dictionary.

4   In Extracts 2 and 4, the writer makes references to the title of the novel, *When the Mountains Roared*. Find these references in the extracts, and write a short explanation of how they link to what is happening in the story. Consider what the writer is suggesting about:

- nature's response to the death of the leopard

- the narrator's reaction to the cub.

5   'This story shows the worst of human attitudes to the natural world'. How far do you agree with this statement about *When the Mountains Roared*? Write a paragraph explaining your view. Use references from the text to support your ideas.

Writing tip

When commenting on a text, it is important to use references and quotations to support your view. Choose specific examples that clearly link to the point you are making.

Summary checklist

- [ ] I can use voice and gesture to convey a character in dialogue.
- [ ] I can write an audioscript based on a prose text, incorporating information from the narrative.
- [ ] I can use context to work out the meaning of unfamiliar words.
- [ ] I can respond to a task, giving my own view and using references to support it.

〉 1.3 The wildness of eagles

In this session, you will:

- identify figurative language in a poem
- summarise information from two texts
- explore the ways language is used in different texts on a similar topic
- organise and take part in a group discussion.

Getting started

What is figurative language? In pairs, talk about the different types of figurative language there are and make a list of terms. Give an example of each one.

'The Eagle'

Read this poem by Alfred, Lord Tennyson.

He **clasps** the **crag** with crooked hands;
Close to the sun in lonely lands,
Ringed with the **azure** world, he stands.

The wrinkled sea beneath him crawls;
He watches from his mountain walls,
And like a thunderbolt he falls.

clasps: holds tightly
crag: a rocky hill or cliff
azure: blue

1   What impression of the eagle does the poet create? Use your own words to describe it.

2   Poets often use **figurative language** techniques such as **simile** and **personification** to present the natural world. They may also use sound-based language techniques such as **alliteration**.

    a   Identify the techniques Tennyson uses in 'The Eagle'. Give examples.

    b   Write a paragraph explaining the effect of the figurative language in the poem. What impact do these techniques have on the reader?

Higher into the Hills

Many texts may explore similar topics and themes, but they do so in different ways. Read this **non-fiction** text in which the writer describes his experiences in Mongolia.

Extract 1

I'd always thought that eagles were beyond human control – they were wild creatures that humans just couldn't tame. On my Mongolian adventure, I discovered the truth.

The next stop on my tour of Mongolia took me higher into the hills. Every July, this beautiful region attracts hundreds of tourists, all amazed to learn about the lives of the Kazakh tribes who live there and their deep bond with the animal world, particularly the eagle.

The 100 000 Kazakhs in Mongolia travel in the summer, living in camps, and in winter they live in houses. I found myself staying with a friendly Kazakh family who were widely respected in the community. This was mainly because Arman, the eldest son, was an expert in training golden eagles. Animals are very important in this area for transport, but it is the eagle – and the ability to tame it – that is a key part of the traditions of these people.

An eagle is a big bird. It builds huge nests in cliff faces, has a two-metre wingspan and can weigh 7 kg. An eagle can fly at speeds of 180 km/hour. It is a fantastic and fearsome hunter. Arman promised me he'd introduce me to Raban, the eagle he had tamed eight years ago, and so there I was in the shimmering

Key words

figurative language: words and phrases used not with their basic meaning but with a more imaginative meaning to create a special effect; figurative language techniques include simile, metaphor and personification

simile: a type of figurative language in which one thing is compared to something else using the words 'as' or 'like'

personification: a type of figurative language in which an object is described as if it has human characteristics

alliteration: use of the same sound, especially consonants, at the beginning of several close-together words

non-fiction: writing that is about real events and facts

early morning light, staring at the impressive hooded eagle sitting on his arm. Arman was an expert. I could see that. I wanted to know how – and why – he had tamed this incredible creature, with its razor-sharp talons and beautiful coat.

3   Look closely at the way the eagle is described in the final paragraph. Then read the poem 'The Eagle' again. Create a table that summarises the appearance and actions of the eagle as it is described in the extract and the poem.

4   Write a paragraph of about 100 words comparing the way language is used to describe the appearance and actions of the eagle in each text. Use relevant quotations to support your points.

Now read the next part of the extract.

Extract 2

Arman explained to me the importance of eagles to the Kazakhs in times gone by. Their great value was their hunting skills. Eagles can be trained to kill animals, which then feed the tribe. Eagles are also an important symbol, he said. They are believed to bring good luck.

I asked Arman how he tamed the bird. It was a skill he learnt from his father. The process is fascinating. First of all, you need to find a bird. This is done by locating a nest way up in the mountains, then taking a young female from it. Female birds are preferred because they are larger so they can catch larger prey. Once the bird has been taken, a hood is put over its head and it is tied down.

This sounds a little cruel to me, but there are some tender aspects to the training. 'I treat my eagle like I treat my own baby,' said Arman. Keeping the eagle calm and happy is very important. Trainers sing and talk to their birds. They communicate. Training an eagle to hunt involves lots of repeated practice and rewards. The human voice is the key. It can take two months before an eagle is ready for hunting.

'Arman truly understands eagles,' noted another family member – and I could see the respect Arman had for this incredible bird. There was a bond that I assumed would last a lifetime. I was wrong. 'We return eagles to the wild after ten years. They are noble. They need freedom eventually,' he explained.

5   Readers choose to read texts for different reasons. Think about *Higher into the Hills* and 'The Eagle'. Which one would you would choose to read:

- for pleasure

- for information

- for research?

Compare your choices with a partner, making sure you explain your reasons clearly.

6   People have different **opinions** about the way humans use animals. Here are two views of the topic:

Key word

opinion: a personal view or judgement about something, not necessarily based on fact or knowledge

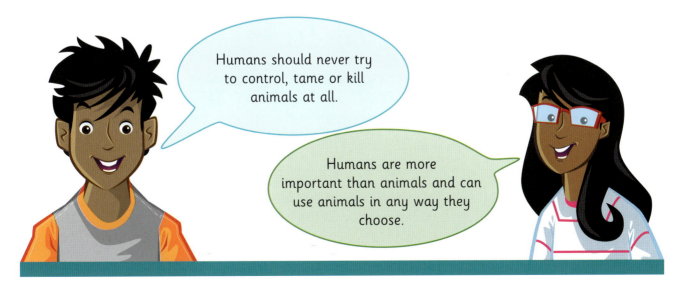

Humans should never try to control, tame or kill animals at all.

Humans are more important than animals and can use animals in any way they choose.

In groups, discuss these views. Use information and examples from *Higher into the Hills*, your own knowledge and any other research you are able to do on the topic. Start by deciding what roles you may need in your group – for example, chairperson or researchers. Try to build on shared ideas and explore points of agreement and disagreement.

Peer assessment

At the end of the discussion, assess what went well and what could be improved:

- How well did you and other members of your group communicate your views?
- Did everybody contribute? If not, why do you think that was?
- On a scale of 1 to 10, how would you judge the listening skills of the group?

Summary checklist

- ☐ I can identify and explore the effects of figurative language in a poem.
- ☐ I can summarise information from two texts concisely and accurately.
- ☐ I can compare the language used in fiction and non-fiction texts on a similar theme.
- ☐ I can work well in a group, taking turns and listening effectively.

> 1.4 The poetry of Tu Fu

In this session, you will:

- identify the main and subsidiary points in an audioscript
- explore the structural features of poetry
- consider how a theme is presented in a range of poems
- analyse how a poet uses language techniques to present theme.

Getting started

In pairs, talk about poems you have studied in school. You should:

- discuss which poems were your favourites and why
- try to remember some lines from these poems.

 1 Tu Fu was a Chinese poet who lived more than 2500 years ago. Listen to the podcast about Tu Fu. As you listen, make notes about the poet's life.

Divide your notes into main points, covering the significant dates and events in his life, and subsidiary points (minor details about his life). Use any method you prefer to make these notes, such as bullet points, a spider diagram or a table.

Listening tip

When listening for main points in a spoken account, focus on dates and key events that stand out as important.

'Loneliness'

Many of Tu Fu's poems explore the link between nature and humans. Read the poem 'Loneliness'.

A hawk hovers in air.
Two white gulls float on the stream.
Soaring with the wind, it is easy
To drop and seize
Birds who foolishly drift with the current.
Where the dew sparkles in the grass,
The spider's web waits for its prey.
The processes of nature resemble the business of men.
I stand alone with ten thousand sorrows.

2 Make brief notes to answer the following questions.

a What does the poet mean when he writes that the birds *foolishly drift with the current*?

b How do you think the spider's web is like *the business of men*?

c How do you interpret the final line? What impression does it give of the narrator's feelings?

3   'In this poem, nature acts as a **symbol** for human behaviour'.
      Write a brief explanation of what this statement means.

Key words

symbol: a literal object that stands for or represents something else

end-stopped: where a line of poetry has a full stop at the end

enjambment: where one line of poetry continues on to the line below

caesura: a break within a line of poetry where either punctuation or the rhythm of the poem indicates a pause

---

Language focus

In poetry, different effects can be created by varying the length of lines and how they are punctuated.

- Some lines of poetry have a punctuation mark at the end – they are **end-stopped** or use a comma.

- Sometimes a poet will use **enjambment** to create a sense of movement or to make the poem sound like a monologue.

- Poets may also decide to use punctuation in the middle of a line (**caesura**) to signify a pause.

Look at this example.

> A hawk hovers in air.
> Two white gulls float on the stream.
> Soaring with the wind, it is easy
> To drop and seize
> Birds who foolishly drift with the current.

The first and second lines are end-stopped. They make the reader pause and focus on the two birds. A sense of stillness is created, as if the hawk and the gulls are waiting.

The next three lines are one sentence split over three lines. The comma after 'wind' creates a caesura. Then enjambment is used to suggest the movement of the birds as they soar, drop and seize. Notice how the punctuation choices are tied to the ideas in the poem.

'Visitors'

4   In pairs, take turns to read 'Visitors' by Tu Fu aloud. As you read, use your voice to convey the tone of the poem.

- Pause when commas and full stops indicate end-stopping or caesura.

- Consider where in the lines the pauses and enjambment fall.

How does this choice of punctuation and position convey the personality and feelings of the narrator? Discuss this in pairs.

I have had asthma for a

Long time. It seems to improve

Here in this house by the river.

It is quiet too. No crowds

Bother me. I am brighter

And more rested. I am happy here.

When someone calls at my thatched hut

My son brings me my straw hat

And I go out and gather

A handful of fresh vegetables.

It isn't much to offer.

But it is given in friendship.

5 In pairs, discuss and compare how the relationship between nature and humans is presented in 'Visitors' and 'Loneliness'. Consider:

- the effect that nature has on humans

- the viewpoints – what can you say about the narrators?

- the purpose of each poem – what is the poet trying to say to the reader?

Reading tip

Comparing two texts means exploring similarities and differences. Use the bullet points or guidance given in tasks to shape your comparison, then focus on similarities at first. You can use the 'Both/but' structure to guide your discussion: 'Both poems … but poem 1…'.

Key word

voice: the way a particular character or narrator speaks or thinks in fiction, or the writer's tone and point of view in non-fiction

6 There are some views on the next page about **voice** and theme in the two poems. Note down some examples from the poems to support or challenge each view, then compare them with a partner.

Tu Fu's poems present nature as aggressive.

Tu Fu's poems show that nature can have a positive effect on humans.

Tu Fu's poems show that nature is beautiful.

The voice of each poem is sad.

The voice of each poem sounds thankful.

- What were the challenges of comparing two poems?
- What advice would you give to someone about to attempt this activity?

'Written on the Wall at Chang's Hermitage'

Now read a final poem by Tu Fu.

It is Spring in the mountains.	You want nothing, although at night
I come alone seeking you.	You can see the aura of gold
The sound of chopping wood echoes	And silver ore all around you.
Between the silent peaks.	You have learned to be gentle
The streams are still icy.	As the mountain deer you have tamed.
There is snow on the trail.	The way back forgotten, hidden
At sunset I reach your grove	Away, I become like you,
In the stony mountain pass.	An empty boat, floating, adrift.

7 a Make notes on how nature is presented in the poem. Think about voice and choice of end-stopping and enjambment.

b Look more closely at the use of language, particularly **aural**, **tactile** and **visual images**. For example, you could explore the feeling of isolation created by the sounds of the chopping wood amid the silence of the mountains.

hermitage: a remote place where a hermit (a religious person) lives alone

Key words

aural image: an image that appeals to the sense of hearing

tactile image: an image that appeals to the sense of touch

visual image: an image that appeals to the sense of sight

c When you have completed your notes, write a 150-word response to this question:

How does Tu Fu present nature in 'Written on the Wall at Chang's Hermitage'?

Remember to use **standard English** in your response, and take care with your handwriting.

Key words

standard English: the most widely accepted form of English that is not specific to a particular region

Summary checklist

☐ I can make clear notes identifying a range of points from an audioscript.

☐ I understand some key structural features of poetry and can comment on their effect.

☐ I can explain how a poet presents a particular theme in a range of poems.

☐ I can analyse how a poet uses language techniques to present theme.

〉 1.5 Destroying the planet

In this session, you will:

- summarise information from two argument texts
- compare how two texts are structured and developed
- explore how writers use connectives
- identify and use formal and informal language.

Getting started

Writers choose the formality of their language depending on many factors. In pairs, discuss any factors that you feel might influence a writer's choice of formal or informal language.

Climate change

In recent years, people have become much more aware of how the climate on our planet is changing. The following texts present two different **arguments** about climate change. **Skim** both texts quickly to get the **gist** of the information and viewpoint in each one. The first is an article from a newspaper for adult readers. The second text is from an online magazine for teenagers.

CLIMATE CHANGE: A NATURAL PROCESS

Our planet is changing. Although it's likely that humans have contributed to these changes, to claim that we are fully responsible isn't true: there are natural forces happening that humans have no influence over, and it's all to do with the way the Earth moves.

Basically, the angle at which our planet is positioned influences the climate. It is true that climate change can alter the way Earth **tilts**. However, it also works the other way: Earth can change its position without any influence from human factors; therefore, it is a natural process.

The way Earth **orbits** the Sun has an effect, too. If the orbit changes, summer and winter temperatures increase; consequently, the North and South Poles travel closer to the Sun. Hence, the **ice caps** melt, which results in rising sea levels.

Changes in weather patterns are also a result of the way Earth changes its position. If the orbit varies, the Sun has more influence and our planet gets warmer. The seasons change too: major storms in Canada and North America used to occur between June and August. Now they take place between August and October.

Climate change is a natural thing. That's not a popular statement, and humans' desire to blame themselves is normal. But there's no need. Although the rising population of the planet does not help, and the way humans use resources is adding to the problem, it isn't all our fault. No. We're victims too.

Article   **About**   **Home**   🔍   ONLINE ARTICLE

WE'RE DESTROYING OUR HOME

OK, so the Earth changes over time. Yes, we know the Ice Age came to an end 12 000 years ago when Earth's orbit changed and the Sun became stronger. Yet what is happening now is much more terrifying! Earth is getting hotter at a faster pace than ever before. We – the human race – are destroying our home. Fact.

How do we know?

For years, scientists have used information from satellites and other sources to examine the data. There's no doubt about it – **greenhouse gases** have increased and this has caused the Earth to heat up. Scientists have examined the effect on ice caps and used information gathered from nature. We are warming our planet ten times faster than ever before!

Here's the evidence:

- The temperature has risen. In the past 200 years, the Earth has got hotter, BUT the past five years have been the hottest ever recorded. FACT.
- Ice is melting – 400 billion tonnes of ice is gone. AND snow is melting earlier in the year than it ever did before. It's terrible news for wildlife. FACT.
- Sea levels are rising. They increased by 25 cm last century, BUT in the past five years, they have gone up – by twice as much again! Sea life suffers and humans suffer. FACT.
- Extreme weather – no one could fail to notice the increase in storms. AND they'll get worse. FACT.

Still don't believe me? Wow! Then ask a scientist. Ninety-seven per cent of them say we're destroying our home.

1   Read both texts again and make notes on:

- who or what is to blame for climate change according to each article
- the main points the writers make in each article.

Before you start, decide on the best way to collate (collect information together) and organise your notes.

2   Now use your notes to consider how these main points are developed and structured in both texts. In pairs, note down:

- at which point in each text the main ideas are placed
- the differences in the use of features such as headings, subheadings and bullet points
- which text you found more appealing and why.

> **greenhouse gases:** gases in the air that trap heat and energy from the Sun

3 **Connectives** can help to structure and sequence an argument. They help to shape the text by clarifying links and emphasising connections between points. For example, the first article uses these features to:

- introduce a new part of the argument

- show contrast

- conclude a point.

Copy and complete the following table.

Example	Purpose
Although it's likely that …	Introduces a contrasting idea.
However, it also works …	
… therefore, it's a natural process	
Hence, the ice caps melt	

Language focus

The type of language a writer uses is linked to the audience and purpose of a text. For example, a headteacher writing to parents about school rules will use **formal language** to indicate their professional status, their respect for their relationship with their audience and also the seriousness of the topic. Formal language choices include the use of:

- complex words, such as specialist terms or more elevated synonyms

- punctuation such as colons and semi-colons

- complex sentence structures.

Writers sometimes use **informal language** to talk to their reader in a friendly way, which establishes a relationship between writer and reader. For example, a text encouraging children to start cycling will be written in a way that is light-hearted and easy to read. Informal language choices include the use of:

- simpler vocabulary and **contractions**

- punctuation such as exclamation marks and dashes

- **simple** and **compound sentences**.

Key words

connective: a word or phrase that links two clauses or sentences together

formal language: the form of English used in more 'serious' texts and situations, such as news reports or official speeches

informal language: a more relaxed form of English, used when speaking or in more casual written texts, such as emails to friends

contraction: two or three words that are combined to make one shorter word with letters left out; the missing letters are indicated by an apostrophe

simple sentence: a sentence with one main clause

compound sentence: a sentence with two main clauses joined by 'and', 'but', 'or'

Continued

Consider the different levels of formality in these examples:

- When considering which phone to purchase, research is paramount.

This is aimed at older adults who are unfamiliar with technology. It uses a **complex sentence** (with a comma to separate the **subordinate clause**) and the complex word *paramount*. The overall effect is of professional, trustworthy advice.

- So – a new phone?! Exciting. Want to compare the latest handsets? Here it goes …

This is written for teenagers and young adults who are familiar with technology. Question marks, exclamations and **ellipsis** are used in a playful way and the sentences are **minor** or simple. The overall effect is light-hearted and friendly to engage the intended audience.

4   Look at the following quotations from the articles on climate change.

A   *If the orbit changes, summer and winter temperatures increase; consequently, the North and South Poles travel closer to the Sun. Hence, the ice caps melt, which results in rising sea levels.*

B   *Sea levels are rising. They increased by 25 cm last century, BUT in the past five years, they have gone up – by twice as much again! Sea life suffers and humans suffer. FACT.*

Write a paragraph of about 100 words comparing the formality of these two extracts. Explain why you think the writers chose these levels of formality and their effects. Comment on features such as:

- choice of words
- use of punctuation
- different sentence types: minor, simple, compound, complex and **compound-complex**.

Key words

complex sentence: a sentence with one main clause and one or more dependent clauses

subordinate clause: in grammar, a clause that cannot form a sentence alone but adds information to the main clause

ellipsis: a set of three dots (…) used to indicate that words have been left out

minor sentence: a sentence that does not contain a main verb

compound-complex sentence: a sentence containing a compound sentence that also has one or more subordinate clauses

5   Rewrite the first article using informal language. You should:

- address the reader in a friendlier tone

- use appropriate language, sentence types, punctuation and connectives.

Writing tip

When writing an argument text, use features such as bullet points and subheadings to guide the reader through your line of argument and make your points really clear.

Summary checklist

☐ I can identify and summarise the main points in more than one text.

☐ I can compare how two texts are structured and developed.

☐ I can explain the purpose of connectives at the start of sentences.

☐ I can understand and use the features of formal and informal language.

> 1.6 Tsunami

In this session, you will:

- use different strategies to work out the meaning of unfamiliar words

- use sources to extend vocabulary about feelings and emotions

- consider how a writer makes grammatical choices for effect

- choose language, grammar and punctuation to create different effects.

Tsunami witness

In this article, adapted from *The Guardian*, the writer describes what happened when a tsunami struck the area of Chile where she lived. A tsunami is a series of large waves triggered by an earthquake. Read the article, paying particular attention to the words that are underlined.

TSUNAMI WITNESS: I SAW THE SEA START TO RISE. THERE WAS TERROR AND ANGUISH

Jocelyn Tordecilla Jorquera lives in Los Vilos, near the <u>epicentre</u> of the earthquake which hit Chile. Here she describes the experience of the ground shaking and the sea coming into her town.

I was at home in Los Vilos with my three children when the house started to shake at 7.55 pm.

The earthquake was very strong and it lasted for an unusually long time – around three minutes. It was longer than any earthquake we had felt before, including the 2010 earthquake.

Out of my window I saw the sea start to rise extremely quickly and come crashing in about two metres high into the coastline. It didn't come in far but the force of the wave was enough to destroy the houses that are at sea level.

We had always been told that tsunami waves take a number of minutes to arrive and in this case it was different – the sea rose immediately.

Since the 2010 earthquake, our family, like all <u>residents</u> of coastal areas in Chile, have had an earthquake plan. We took immediate action and went into the most secure room of our house – the main bedroom, which after the 2010 earthquake we <u>constructed</u> in light material, in wood, as a <u>precaution</u>.

And then we <u>evacuated</u> the house on foot to the community's <u>designated</u> secure zone – a hill less than a kilometre from the town that's about 20 metres above sea level.

It only took us about 10 minutes to get there but there was sheer terror and <u>anguish</u> – people were running and no one knew what was going to happen. Some people were on foot, others fled in their cars.

More than seven hours later, we're still here, with lots of people and above 40 vehicles, because the aftershocks are continuing. There's more people from the town <u>congregating</u> further up the hill.

My husband went back to our house to get our car, and my children, aged 5, 10 and 13, are now asleep in it.

It is very quiet now. The electricity has just cut out in most of the town, and it's in darkness.

Language focus

There are several ways of working out the meaning of unfamiliar words. You could use:

- context: looking at the words around it and the overall topic to make a sensible guess at the meaning

- **morphology**: looking at the shape of the word – that is, seeing if it has a **root word**, a **prefix** or a **suffix**, and using your knowledge of those to work out the whole word

- **etymology**: looking up the origins of a word to discover its possible meaning.

Sometimes a combination of methods will help you. For example, look at this sentence:

- He stared down the dark, lonely street in trepidation.

What does 'trepidation' mean?

- context: you may notice that the street sounds scary, so you might guess that trepidation means something like 'a feeling of fear'.

- morphology: you may notice that trepidation uses the suffix '-ation', which you know refers to a state or quality. From this, you could guess that the word is a type of feeling.

- etymology: you might research the origins of the word and discover that it comes from the Latin word *trepido*, meaning 'to shake'.

Key words

morphology: the study of how words are formed and their relationship with other words

root word: the basic form of a word that other words with related meanings are based on

prefix: letters added to the beginning of a word to make a new word with a different meaning

suffix: letters added to the end of a word to make a new word with a different meaning

etymology: the origins of a word

1 Work out the meanings of the underlined words in the article using one of the strategies described. Create a **glossary** for the article with definitions of all these words.

2 Read the article again. As you read, track the times and the **sequence** of main events. Create a timeline to show the order of events.

3 In pairs, discuss the emotions that the narrator and her family might have experienced at different points during the day.
Use a thesaurus and online sources to write a list of interesting words to precisely define various feelings. Write these against the relevant times and events on your list or timeline.

4 Writers choose their words carefully, using them in particular ways to create different meanings and effects. Word choice works closely with other choices, such as grammar and punctuation. Look at this sentence:

Some people fled on foot, others in their cars.

Now look at the way this sentence has been rewritten below to create a different effect:

They sprinted in absolute fear. That's what they did. Men, women, children: all of them ran for their lives. Others – the lucky ones – scrambled into cars and hurtled away as fast as they possibly could.

Make notes on the different choices of words, grammar and punctuation. What effect is created?

5 Another way to create different effects is to rearrange **clauses**. Look at the first sentence of the article and note how the narrator begins with information about her home and family:

I was at home in Los Vilos with my three children when the house started to shake at 7.55pm.

Here is the same information presented in a different order:

When the house started to shake, I was at home in Los Vilos with my three children. It was 7.55pm.

What effect is created by reordering the clauses? Does it change the emphasis? Does it make the opening more or less dramatic? Discuss your thoughts in pairs.

Key words

glossary: an alphabetical list of words or phrases from a text, with their meanings

sequence: the order of events in a story

Reading tip

When tracking the main events in a text, skim read to identify times, days and significant moments.
Note down this information using a bullet-point list or a timeline.

Key word

clause: a group of words that contains a verb

6   Write a new version of the final paragraph (*It is very quiet now …*), making different choices of words, punctuation and grammar. You should aim to create the same feeling of tension and fear that the original has. Write about 100 words.

Self-assessment

Reread your paragraph. How effective were your choices of language, grammar and punctuation? Which ones did you feel were most effective in creating tension and fear?

Place a tick under red, amber or green in a copy of the table to show the effectiveness of your choices.

	🔴	🟠	🟢
Language			
Grammar			
Punctuation			

Redraft your paragraph to improve it.

Summary checklist

- [ ] I can use a variety of strategies effectively to work out the meaning of unfamiliar words.
- [ ] I can use precise vocabulary to describe feelings and emotions related to events.
- [ ] I can comment on how a writer creates detail and effects through grammatical choices.
- [ ] I can create different meanings through choice of language, grammar and punctuation.

Check your progress

Answer these questions.

1. What is the difference in effect between a present tense verb and past tense verb? Give some examples.

2. Describe the main differences between a drama script and prose writing.

3. Give some examples of figurative language.

4. Explain the impact of the placement of punctuation choices in poems – what effect is created by end-stopping, enjambment and caesura?

5. Give an example of a compound-complex sentence.

6. Explain two strategies for working out the meaning of unfamiliar words.

Project

In this unit you have explored the relationship between nature and humans. Sometimes that relationship is positive; sometimes it is destructive.

Think about how the relationship between nature and humans is represented in books, poems, pictures, TV shows and films. In groups, collect examples that show the relationship in different ways. Find paragraphs, lines or pictures that present a memorable image of the interaction between humans and nature.

Once you have collected your examples, think of an interesting way to display them. You could create a wall display in your classroom, compile them to make a book, create a visual presentation or upload them to your school website.

Afterwards, give a presentation about your collection to the class. Each group member should talk about some of the things you chose. Remember to explain clearly why you chose each item and what you feel it shows about the human–nature relationship. Speak clearly and with enthusiasm to engage your listeners.

2 'Grandmother's Song'

In this unit, you will study a short story called 'Grandmother's Song' by Barbara Soros. You will look at the structure of the story, the themes it explores and the ways in which it could be interpreted. You will also consider the influence of the story's cultural context.

> 2.1 Life in the village

In this session, you will:

- consider how a writer establishes the setting of a story
- explore how sentence openings are used to guide a reader
- explore interpretations of figurative language in character descriptions
- analyse how a writer combines techniques for effect.

Getting started

Stories start in different ways. Some begin by describing the setting, some open with dialogue and others dive straight into the action. With a partner, discuss examples of story openings you have read. Which ones did you prefer and why?

'Grandmother's Song' by Barbara Soros is a short story about a grandmother and her granddaughter who live in a village in Mexico. Read the first part of the story.

Extract 1

In the heart of Mexico, hawks soar above high mountains and swoop down to gentle slopes of corn below. There on glistening rocks, **iguanas** rest beneath the hot, tropical sun. **Toucans** chatter to ring-tailed cats perched in emerald green trees. All through these hills, puma run, grey foxes search for chickens and wolves call to each other in the night.

In a village at the foot of these mountains, a grandmother lived with her granddaughter. They planted corn, tomatoes and sunflowers in the spring and watched as new green shoots sprang from the earth. They gathered milk-white **lilies** in the summer and put them in baskets on their backs and took them to market. At harvest time, they decorated tall stalks of maize at the corn festival, to give thanks for the year's grain.

Grandmother stood proud and tall. Her **downy** cheeks stretched smooth and plump across wide cheekbones. Her eyes were deep and warm and brown, and though they were sad, they were also kind. Powerful legs and sturdy feet rooted her to the earth, like an ancient tree. Her arms were strong and her hands graceful, with long, fine fingers.

iguana: a type of lizard

toucan: a brightly coloured bird

lilies: funnel-like flowers

downy: covered in fine, soft hair

1 Make notes on how the writer presents the **setting** of Mexico in this extract.

2 Writers often choose specific words or phrases for their sentence opening. These help the reader make links within a text. In the first paragraph of 'Grandmother's Song', three sentence openings include a location: 'Mexico', 'rocks' and 'hills'. They also contain the **prepositions** 'in', 'on' and 'through'. These show the link between the location and the scenery or animals in it.

Look at the second paragraph of the extract. At the start of each sentence, the writer repeats the **pronoun** 'they', followed by a verb such as *planted* or *gathered*. In pairs, find and list these phrases, then discuss the effect of the pattern.

Key words

setting: the location where a story takes place

preposition: a word or group of words used before a noun or pronoun to show place, direction, time, etc. (for example, 'above', 'below', 'under')

pronoun: a word that stands in for a noun to avoid repetition; pronouns can be subject personal pronouns (e.g. 'I', 'you'), object personal pronouns (e.g. 'him', 'them') or possessive pronouns (e.g. 'mine', 'ours')

Reading tip

When reading the opening of a story, think about how the setting is introduced. What hint might this give you about the story? Does it lead you to expect a happy tale? Does it suggest danger?

Now read the next part of the story, which introduces the character of the granddaughter.

Extract 2

Granddaughter was as delicate as the **blossoms** of a **jacaranda** tree. Her wide-open eyes shone black and clear. Her tiny, bow lips looked as if she ate strawberries all day long. Granddaughter loved to explore and to imagine. She often played in the fields and forests on her own, but as she played she trembled. For she was afraid of the dark shadows and of the cries of the animals and of anything that was new and strange.

If she heard anything, even the scamper of an **ocelot** on the upper branches, her heart fluttered and her stomach churned and she shook from the inside out and the outside in, like dry leaves rustling in a sack on a windy afternoon.

One day, trembling granddaughter met an **armadillo**. It was just an ordinary armadillo running across her path, but she shook and shivered as though it were a huge bear with sharp claws and gnashing teeth. After that, every passing shadow seemed to be the fearsome creature following her home.

blossoms: flowers on a tree or bush
jacaranda: a tree with blue flowers
ocelot: a small wild cat
armadillo: a mammal covered in bony plates

Language focus

Writers use figurative language, such as simile and **metaphor**, to give readers a way of understanding characters that goes beyond describing them in a **literal** way. Figurative language opens up different meanings which add complexity to descriptions. For example, if a man is described using the simile 'like the sun hidden by a cloud', this could mean:

- the man looks miserable but is actually happy
- the man brings a positive attitude to bad situations
- the man's positive attitude is spoilt by the world he lives in.

When thinking about the meanings that figurative language such as similes and metaphors create, always read them in the context of what you already know about the character and the story. Ask yourself what the language says about the character's attitudes and how these attitudes are shown elsewhere in the story.

Key words

metaphor: a type of comparison that describes one thing as if it is something else
literal: describing something in a straightforward way, using the original, direct meaning of words

3 In Extracts 1 and 2, the writer uses similes to describe the grandmother and granddaughter. For example, she uses these words to describe grandmother:

Powerful legs and sturdy feet rooted her to the earth, like an ancient tree.

Read this paragraph, in which a learner explains what this simile shows.

> The writer uses a simile to compare how the grandmother stands like an 'ancient tree', which shows the grandmother's strength – old trees are usually very large. Old trees also have big roots, which suggests that grandmother has many life experiences and also that she is trustworthy and unlikely to break easily. The word 'ancient' also shows her wisdom – it suggests that she has learnt many things and will be able to use her experiences to help her granddaughter.

Using this response as a model, write a paragraph explaining what the writer means by the following simile: *Granddaughter was as delicate as the blossoms of a jacaranda tree.*

Peer assessment

Swap your writing with a partner.

- What interpretation of the simile has your partner decided on?
- Did you interpret it in the same way?
- Do you agree with their interpretation?
- What could they add to develop their explanation?

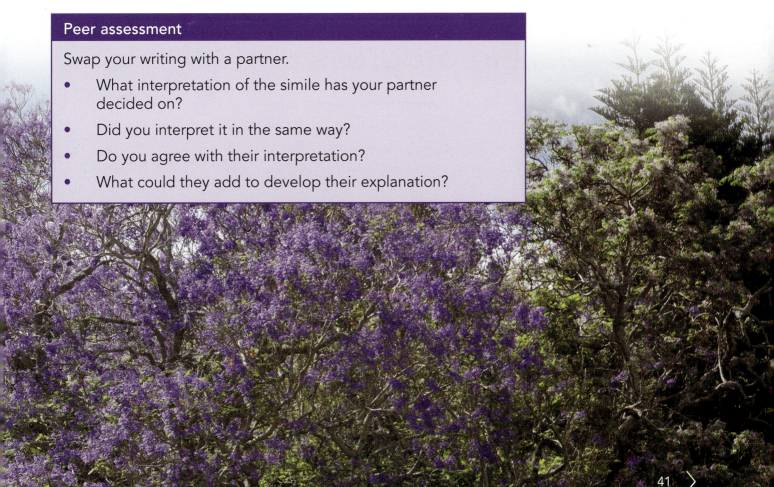

4   In 'Grandmother's Song', the writer uses **contrast** as a structural device. On your own, make a list of the similarities and differences between grandmother and granddaughter. When you have finished, use your notes to make a **prediction** about how the characters might change as the story progresses.

5   The writer combines structural and language techniques, including contrast and figurative language, to show the character of the granddaughter. Write a paragraph explaining the methods the writer uses to show how granddaughter is innocent and scared.

Key words

contrast: placing two characters or things together in order to highlight their differences

prediction: an idea about what might happen in the future

Summary checklist

- [ ] I can comment on how writers structure story openings to establish setting.
- [ ] I can explain the purpose and effect of particular sentence openings.
- [ ] I understand how simile and metaphor can be used to reveal character.
- [ ] I can describe how a writer combines structural and language techniques to show what a character is like.

› 2.2 Making progress

In this session, you will:

- trace the links between plot and character in a story
- explore how direct speech is used to reveal character
- discuss different views about a story
- write about the purpose and effect of a structural device.

Getting started

What is the difference between language and structure? In pairs, make a list of structural features that are common in fiction stories. For example, consider the order that information can be revealed and how the writer makes links between different parts of a story.

Read the next part of 'Grandmother's Song'.

Extract 3

When grandmother heard the door creak open, she ran to her granddaughter and scooped her up in her arms, hugging her. Then she settled granddaughter on her great, wide lap and gently stroked her. She stroked her head and her slender back, and as she stroked, she sang, 'Oh, my little one, I can feel your young heart beating so. I can feel trembling inside your belly. I can hear fear inside your bones.'

She stroked and stroked and then continued, 'The world is a frightening place for those who cannot trust. So I am stroking trust into you, the trust I feel and the trust my grandmother felt and her grandmother before her.'

Granddaughter felt her immense warmth entering her body, and as the sun set behind the house, slowly the trembling eased and she fell asleep.

The next day, a group of children surprised trembling granddaughter as she played at the roadside. They ran over the hill right towards her, gleefully laughing and shouting. 'Which way to the river?' they called. Instead of running away, granddaughter pointed to the left without her finger wavering, even though she was shaking inside.

That evening, trembling granddaughter told her grandmother what had happened. Grandmother smiled. 'That's progress!' she declared. She lifted granddaughter onto her lap and stroked her like a cat, then she began to sing, 'Listen carefully, my little one. I can feel trembling in your belly. I can hear fear inside your bones. The world is a frightening place for those without courage, but today you showed you were brave by pointing the way even though you wanted to run.'

1   All stories have a **plot** – a series of connected events that show how characters and situations change. Copy and complete the following table to show what happens in each paragraph of Extract 3 and what it reveals about the characters.

> **Key word**
>
> **plot:** the main events of a story, film, novel or play in sequence from beginning to end

Paragraph	What happens	What it shows
1	Granddaughter returns; grandmother hugs her, sings to her, tells her she knows she is scared.	Grandmother cares deeply for the girl; understands her. Granddaughter still has to get over her feelings of fear.
2		
3		
4		
5		

2 Look at the words the writer uses to describe the actions and qualities of grandmother and granddaughter. Make notes on the effect these words create – what impression do you get of the characters?

3 Grandmother's voice is very distinctive, and her words help to reveal her character. In pairs, look at grandmother's **direct speech** in Extract 3. What do you learn about her character? In your answer, consider:

- the words she uses to refer to her granddaughter

- repeated words

- phrases she uses that are similar to one another.

Now read the next part of the story.

Extract 4

Some time later, a young hummingbird fell from a nest in the garden and broke its wing. Instead of running away, trembling granddaughter walked towards the little bird and picked it up. Its body was shaking even more than her own. She could feel its tiny, fluttering heart and its warm, feathery tummy. She held the hummingbird with the same tenderness as her grandmother had held her, and carried it inside.

Grandmother knew how to look after hurt animals. Together they made a little nest of cloth and straw in a box and fed the bird.

Grandmother's smile spread across her face and lit up her eyes. 'Certainly, this is progress!' she exclaimed. And while the hummingbird slept, grandmother took trembling granddaughter on her broad lap and sang to her, 'My little one, listen well. I can feel trembling in your belly. I can hear fear inside your bones. The world is a frightening place for those who cannot help others. Today you helped a tiny, frightened creature and discovered your gift of healing.'

All through the night, she held her beloved grandchild safe on her comfortable lap and sang, 'This is my gift that I am stroking into you. It is also a gift of my grandmother and of her grandmother before her.'

4   Read these three views about the hummingbird and its importance in the story. Discuss these views in small groups. Which views do you agree with? Remember to take turns, listen carefully to the opinions of other group members and to explore shared ideas.

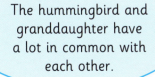
The writer includes the hummingbird in the story to show how much granddaughter has developed.

When the granddaughter cares for the hummingbird, it shows the positive effect that grandmother has had.

The hummingbird and granddaughter have a lot in common with each other.

Speaking tip

When asked to comment on different views of a text, always try to find evidence from the text to support or challenge each idea. This will help you draw conclusions and explain them clearly.

5   Write a 100-word paragraph explaining the use of the hummingbird as a structural device. Think about why the writer introduces it at this point in the story. Use evidence from the text to support your view.

- How confident do you feel when writing about structural features in fiction?
- What might help you to become even better at writing about *how* and *why* writers structure their stories in certain ways?

Summary checklist

- ☐ I can identify how events in a story reveal information about characters.
- ☐ I can explain how a character's words tell the reader what they are like.
- ☐ I can listen and contribute effectively during a discussion about a story.
- ☐ I can explain the purpose and effect of a structural device, using evidence to support my ideas.

> 2.3 Growing up

In this session, you will:

- perform an unseen text in groups
- consider how dialogue and reporting verbs convey character and voice
- comment on the effects of figurative language
- discuss story structures, including endings.

Getting started

When writing dialogue, it is easy to fall into the habit of using the verb 'said' when in fact there are many more descriptive verbs that would reveal more about your character's personality and mood.

In pairs, write a list of alternative words for 'said'. Discuss the effect of each of these alternatives. What do they suggest about the situation or the speaker?

Read the next part of 'Grandmother's Song'.

1 Perform this part of the story in groups of four. Divide the roles between you: narrator, granddaughter, merchant and grandmother. As you perform the dialogue and the narration, focus on:

- speaking confidently and with expression
- using gesture, movement and tone of voice to convey the **mood**.

> **Key word**
>
> **mood:** the feeling created by the words, sounds and images in a text

Extract 5

One afternoon, trembling granddaughter was browsing at a market stall when the merchant accused a child of stealing something he had not taken. She watched the angry face of the merchant as he jabbed his finger at the child. Though her heart beat loudly, trembling granddaughter approached the man and said, 'This boy did not take anything; I have watched him. Please do not scream at him.'

The merchant just snarled in reply, so she asked, 'How much money have you lost?'

'Ten pesos,' he muttered. The girl reached into her pocket and gave him all her spending money.

'Ah, this is real progress!' grandmother remarked as trembling granddaughter told her tale, gasping for breath, as she had run all the way home.

Then grandmother took her beloved grandchild on her broad lap and stroked her for a very long time. 'My little one, listen well,' she sang. 'The world is a frightening place for people without dignity. Today you showed your dignity, when you stood tall between the earth and sky. To that I add the dignity I have been given, the dignity of my grandmother and of her grandmother before her.'

> **Speaking tip**
>
> When performing an unseen text, try to read ahead slightly as you are performing, so you know what is coming next. Vary the volume and **pace** of your speech to emphasise key parts of the text you are performing. Choose your actions to suit the voice of your character.

> **Key word**
>
> **pace:** the speed at which someone speaks or how quickly events take place in a story

- What are the challenges of reading an unseen text aloud?
- What advice would you give to another learner who wants to improve this skill?

Language focus

One way to show the attitude and feelings of a character in your writing is by choosing **reporting verbs** carefully to describe how the character speaks. Different verbs can suggest particular qualities. For example, using the verb 'bellowed' may suggest that the character has a confident personality or is in an angry mood. Look at these examples used to report direct speech:

- 'Leave me alone,' he begged.

- 'Leave me alone!' he yelled.

- 'Can I ask you to give me ten minutes alone?' he whispered.

Each reporting verb creates a different impression of the person speaking. The first example suggests that the speaker is weak or weary. The second suggests the speaker is angry. Notice how the third example could suggest two quite different feelings – the speaker may be upset or he may be speaking in a low, threatening way.

Key words

reporting verb: a verb that conveys the action of speaking – used with both direct and reported speech

2   Explain how the writer uses reporting verbs and language to suggest the characters of the merchant and the grandmother in these examples.

   a   *The merchant just snarled in reply …*
   b   *'Ten pesos,' he muttered.*
   c   *'Ah, this is real progress!' grandmother remarked …*
   d   *'My little one, listen well,' she sang.*

3   In the first two sentences of Extract 5, the merchant accuses the boy of stealing. Write this event out as a paragraph using dialogue to show the conversation between the merchant and the boy. Think carefully about each character's voice, as part of their personality and under these particular circumstances.

Peer assessment

In groups of three, read your paragraphs aloud.

- What techniques have each of you used to create the voices?

- How successfully does each dialogue reflect the two voices?

Now read the next part of the story.

Extract 6

Trembling granddaughter sensed a strange pride pour through her body. She felt bigger and stronger than usual and her face felt vibrant and warm.

How many times did grandmother stroke her granddaughter? How many times did she sing to her? I do not know. But I do know that she did it many, many times, for many weeks and for many years. She stroked trust and courage, skill and dignity into trembling granddaughter. And her song went so deep that it moved through the girl's flesh into her muscles, into her blood, into her heart, and finally into her bones.

Granddaughter grew up to be trusting and trustworthy, generous and kind. No one even remembered that she once ran from armadillos. Soon she grew up into a strong and confident woman, rich in laughter, delighting in everything around her.

Now granddaughter had children of her own, but still on occasions, she laid her head in grandmother's lap. She understood well the language of grandmother's hands. And so, as the old woman's fingers traced their familiar path, granddaughter smiled and closed her eyes.

4   How does the writer use figurative language in this part of the story? Copy and complete the table to identify the figurative language and explain its meaning and effect.

Example of figurative language	Meaning and effect
Trembling granddaughter sensed a strange pride pour through her body.	Personification is used to compare the feeling of pride to a liquid – 'pour' suggests a large, fast-moving quantity. The effect of this is to show the reader how much the granddaughter has developed from a hesitant girl to one whose positive emotions now move freely and quickly through her.
She stroked trust and courage, skill and dignity into trembling granddaughter.	
She understood well the language of grandmother's hands.	

5   The story develops around the progress the granddaughter makes in overcoming her fears. Look back at the extracts so far. In pairs:

   •   identify the key events that show her development from a scared child to a confident adult

   •   make sketches to show these key events

   •   discuss the effect of each event and how they relate to each other.

6   Read these two possible endings for the story.

   A: Granddaughter's child is also fearful. Granddaughter uses the things she has learnt from grandmother to help her own child overcome her fears.

   B: Granddaughter decides to use the knowledge she has gained from her grandmother to help the people of the village. She teaches others how to overcome their fears.

   a   In groups, discuss the two endings. How are they similar and different? Which ending do you think is most likely and why? Refer to the key events from earlier in the story that you identified in Activity 5 to support your ideas.

   b   On your own, write a different ending to the story. Think about what might happen to the characters. Will you choose a happy or sad ending?

Summary checklist

☐   I can perform an unseen text with expression, showing evidence of reading ahead.

☐   I understand how dialogue and reporting verbs can convey character and voice and can use them effectively in my own writing.

☐   I can identify the meaning and effect of figurative language.

☐   I can chart the development of a character and use this to discuss how a story might end.

> 2.4 Climbing the mountains alone

In this session, you will:

- identify and explore the effect of **explicit** and **implicit information**
- discuss views on the ending of a story
- consider how different cultural beliefs affect how readers react to stories
- express a personal response to a story.

Getting started

What does the phrase 'cultural beliefs' mean? How might your own beliefs affect the way you react to stories and other people's ideas and attitudes? Discuss your ideas in pairs.

Read the next part of 'Grandmother's Song'.

Extract 7

In time, grandmother grew old and more frail. So granddaughter attended to her, coming at dawn to light the fire and to boil water for tea. She cooked for her and she washed and brushed her fine, silver hair. She massaged her well-worn feet, gently rubbing every single toe. She took grandmother's loving hands in hers and massaged her old stiff fingers. Sometimes, but now less frequently, they walked together across the village, through the valley into the mountains, laughing and singing together. And wherever the ground was uneven, granddaughter offered grandmother her arm.

One night in a dream, granddaughter saw grandmother walking up the mountains alone. She wanted to walk with her, but grandmother turned and raised her hand. 'I have to go on alone,' she said, with a quiet smile in her eyes.

The next morning, granddaughter went to grandmother's house as usual. But when she went to wake her, grandmother's body was cold and her face free from worry.

Granddaughter dropped to her knees. Grief struck as quickly and precisely as lightning.

She felt her heart flutter and her stomach churn, just as they had when she was a child. She trembled from head to toe, like cedar branches in a raging storm. How could she live without her beloved grandmother? Her heart opened like a river and tears soaked her face and spilled onto her chest. She doubled over in despair and sobs welled up from her belly and her bones.

1   In pairs, list the things from the first paragraph that the granddaughter does for the grandmother. Next to each one, note down how it links to earlier parts of the story.

2   In this part of the story, the writer uses many images of nature.

    a   What do you think the image of the grandmother climbing the mountains alone symbolises?

    b   List the three images from nature that show the granddaughter's grief.

    c   Why do you think the writer has used these images to describe grief? What effect do they create for the reader?

Now read the final part of the story.

Extract 8

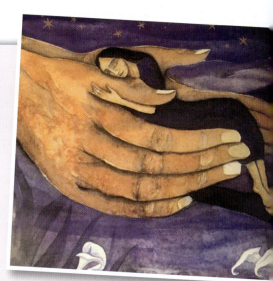

'My little one,' grandmother's voice filled the room. 'My little one, listen well.' Granddaughter felt strong, warm hands tenderly stroking her back. These invisible hands felt more immense than grandmother's earthly hands. They stroked well-being into her from her head to her toes, up her front and down her back. She felt the hands pick her up and cradle her and rock her back and forth as if she were an infant. And granddaughter felt warmth entering her heart, her belly and her bones. Just as suddenly as her sobbing had begun, it ceased. She felt a lightness in her heart and strength in her limbs. She was standing on her feet now, stroking the cheeks and the forehead of her dear, dead grandmother.

Granddaughter has become a grandmother many times now. She has taken her children and her grandchildren across her own broad lap. She has cradled them with her strong, skilful arms, she has laughed and cried with them, she has sung to them and she has stroked them, whispering, 'My little ones, listen well. Grandmother's spirit is all around us. She is in the wind and in the trees. She is in the valleys and the hills. She is always there when we are with warm friends, when we taste delicious food, and whenever there is carefree laughter or salty tears are shed. No matter where we are, grandmother is never far away. And whenever we need her, we can simply shut our eyes and feel her holding us so very close.'

3   Was the prediction you made about the ending in Session 2.3 correct? Here are two learners' views about the ending. In pairs, discuss whether or not you agree with these views. Give reasons for your ideas and explain any other views you have on the ending.

This is a very sad story. It reminds us that people we love are not with us for ever. It seems really cruel that the love between the two characters has to end. The grief that the granddaughter feels is very deep. I liked the story, but found the ending too sad.

This story seems to end sadly, but it is uplifting. The granddaughter is upset, but she learns that the memory of her grandmother will always be with her. Therefore, the story is reassuring. I like the way it ended – it reminds me that life goes on and love never ends.

 4   Stories often reflect the writer's culture – ideas from the time and place the story was written may be found in the text. People around the world have different attitudes to life and death. 'Grandmother's Song' reflects aspects of Mexican culture. Listen to the audio track of Miguel discussing Mexican traditions and answer the questions.

a   What two backgrounds does Miguel say Mexicans come from?

b   What does Miguel mean when he says the cathedral 'takes his breath away'?

c   What do Mexicans celebrate on 16 September?

d Name three things that Mexicans do on 16 September to celebrate, according to Miguel.

e Name two instruments that are used in Mariachi bands.

f What does Miguel mean when he says 'When I listen to Mariachi music, I feel a strong connection to the past'?

5 When you read a story from a culture different to your own, your thoughts and feelings about it may vary. In pairs, discuss how you react to the ideas in 'Grandmother's Song'. This is a complex topic, so you will need to choose language carefully to explain your views. Remember to listen to your partner as well as to contribute to the discussion.

Self-assessment

When you have finished your discussion, assess how well you think it went:

- How effective was the discussion?
- Did you explain and understand the ideas?
- Did you use appropriate language in your discussion?

6 Write a 150-word personal response to 'Grandmother's Song', explaining your views and opinions. This could include:

- what you enjoyed about the story
- how you reacted to what happened in the story
- what was the main point the writer was making about family life.

Summary checklist

- [ ] I can identify explicit and implicit information and comment on their meaning and effects.
- [ ] I can discuss different views about the ending of a story and give my own opinion.
- [ ] I can understand how different cultural beliefs affect how we react to stories.
- [ ] I can write a personal response to a story, including an interpretation of its meaning.

Listening tip

When listening to people speak about topics that are new to you, remember to identify **facts** first of all, but also listen to the views and attitudes being expressed to gain a deeper understanding of meanings.

Key word

fact: something that is known to have happened or exist

Writing tip

When responding to a task, be mindful of who you are writing for and why. This will help you to decide how formal the language you use should be. When writing about serious topics or giving personal responses which your teacher will read, use formal standard English.

› 2.5 Celebrating grandparents

> **In this session, you will:**
>
> - explore themes and ideas across more than one text
> - identify and summarise the main and subsidiary points in a text
> - write a biographical account.

> **Getting started**
>
> What do you understand by the word 'theme'? Think of some stories or films you know and identify the main themes they explore. Discuss your ideas in pairs.

1   One way to interpret stories is to consider the themes they contain. One of the key themes in 'Grandmother's Song' is the importance of human contact. At the end of the book, the writer talks about this theme, which she refers to as 'the power of touch'.

Read what she says, then answer the following questions.

a   What does the writer mean when she says when we touch our children *we imprint both the past and the future*?

b   What might she mean when she says, *When children are listened to in this way, they can learn to know what is in their bones*?

Extract 9

When grandmother touches granddaughter she brings to her the love and wisdom of generations. When we touch our children we imprint both the past and the future. In our touch we carry the way we have been touched.

When grandmother listens she listens beneath the fear into the bones of her grandchild. This is the kind of listening that is needed for children to know they are being received and respected. When children are listened to in this way, they can learn to know what is in their bones.

2   The theme of human contact is developed throughout the story. Here are six quotations on this theme. In pairs, consider the way touch is shown in these quotations, relating them to the writer's comments on the theme of touch.

- *she ran to her granddaughter and scooped her up in her arms, hugging her.*
- *She lifted granddaughter onto her lap and stroked her like a cat, then she began to sing.*
- *She held the hummingbird with the same tenderness as her grandmother had held her.*
- *She stroked trust and courage, skill and dignity into trembling granddaughter.*
- *She took grandmother's loving hands in hers and massaged her old stiff fingers.*
- *whenever we need her, we can simply shut our eyes and feel her holding us so very close.*

3   Here are some other themes covered in 'Grandmother's Song'. Find quotations from the story that illustrate each theme.

- Human growth: In the story, the granddaughter is very fearful at the start but develops into a confident woman with the encouragement of her grandmother.
- The cycle of life: The story shows how one generation helps another and that life has repeating patterns – people are born, learn things and then pass them on to their own children.
- Memory: The writer reminds us that even when people die, they live on in our memories.
- The wisdom of older people: Grandmother is presented as a wise woman who knows exactly how to help granddaughter. The story gives a very positive view of older people.

4   Think of a book you have read that explores one of the themes in Activity 3. What similarities and differences can you see in the way the texts explore the theme? Discuss your ideas in pairs.

- How easy did you find it to compare texts?
- What methods did you use?

Reading tip

When looking through a full story for quotations, use your **scanning** skills. Read the text quickly and search for key words connected to the information you are trying to find.

Key word

scan: to look through a text quickly to find particular details

The Secret Life of my Grandfather

'Grandmother's Song' told the story of an older person in a particular culture. Now you are going to read a different type of text about an older person – the opening to a **biography** about someone's grandfather. As you read the text, think about what are the main points the writer makes and what are subsidiary points.

Key word

biography: an account of someone's life

Reading tip

When identifying main points and subsidiary points in a text, use different coloured highlighters or organise your notes into a table.

The old man by the fire

As he sits hunched by the fire, it's hard to imagine my grandfather as anything other than a quiet old man. But things aren't always as they appear. Seventy-five years ago, he was a young man living in Poland. I've seen photographs from that time. He's tall, handsome and looks great in his Polish army uniform – the one he got married in. He was a captain in the army, but when the Russians took over the part of Poland he lived in, he had to make a decision: should he stay in Poland with his family and risk danger, or should he take his new wife — my grandmother — and start a new life abroad?

A long journey

In the end, he did the only thing he could. He helped his wife and both their families start a new life in England. He used all his money to buy train tickets and made sure they got away safely. By this time, Poland had become a dangerous place, but my grandfather stayed there alone for a week after his family left before making his way across Europe. Sometimes he caught trains, sometimes he got lifts in cars, but most of the time he walked. It took him one month to reach England.

5   Summarise the content of these paragraphs. Use a table with two columns to show:

•   the main points (the main things you learn about the grandfather's life)

•   the subsidiary points (smaller details about the grandfather's life).

6   Write a positive account of an older relative, aimed at other adults in your family. Write 200 words.

•   Start by making notes and planning what you want to say about them, for example, by using a spider diagram, bullet points or a table.

- Then, think about how you will structure your writing. What order will you reveal the information?

- Choose appropriate layout features such as subheadings and pictures to present your writing in an effective way.

- Use standard English and formal language.

- Write **fluently** in clear handwriting.

Self-assessment

When you have drafted your text, read it through, considering the following questions:

- Is your structure clear and effective?

- Have you used standard English and an appropriate level of formality?

- Are your grammar and punctuation accurate?

Edit your work to improve it.

Summary checklist

☐ I can explain how themes and ideas are developed in a text and how they relate to other texts.

☐ I can identify and summarise the main and subsidiary points in a text.

☐ I can write, evaluate and edit a biographical account.

> 2.6 Comparing texts

In this session, you will:

- compare and comment on texts with similar themes
- explore the conventions of folk tales
- make a reasoned choice about which stories to read.

What are the differences between the way information is presented in poems and stories? In pairs, make a list of these differences.

'Jessie Emily Schofield'

The poem 'Jessie Emily Schofield' by Judy Williams explores similar themes to 'Grandmother's Song'. Both texts are about the relationship between a grandmother and granddaughter, and both include ideas about human touch and memory. In the poem, the narrator describes washing her grandmother's hair. Read the poem in pairs.

I used to wash my grandmother's hair,

When she was old and small

And walked with a frame

Like a learning child.

She would turn off her hearing aid

And bend into the water,

Holding the edge of the sink with long fingers;

I would pour warm cupfuls over her skull

And wonder what it could be like

In her deaf head with eighty years of life.

Hers was the softest hair I ever felt,

Wedding dress silk on a widow;

But there is a photo of her

Sitting swathed in hair

That I imagine chestnut from the black and white,

Long enough to sit on.

Her wet head felt delicate as a birdskull

Worn thin by waves of age,

As she stood bent,

My mother's mother under my hands.

swathed: covered
chestnut: a red-brown colour

1   In pairs, discuss the main ideas in the poem. Look at:

- where ideas about touch are shown and what they reveal about the relationship

- how ideas about the past are shown and what they reveal about time and people.

2   Summarise the development of ideas about people changing in this poem and in 'Grandmother's Song'.

a   Write down lines from 'Jessie Emily Schofield' that show how the grandmother has changed over time.

b   Briefly summarise the events in 'Grandmother's Song' that show how the granddaughter changes.

3   Compare the ideas and information about the granddaughters in 'Grandmother's Song' and 'Jessie Emily Schofield'. Make some notes using these prompts:

- How does each granddaughter feel about her grandmother?

- Do both granddaughters develop or learn things? If so, what?

4   Even when exploring the same theme, different writers use language in different ways. Look at these quotations describing the age and appearance of each grandmother:

- *Her wet head felt delicate as a birdskull*
  Worn thin by waves of age,…

  (From 'Jessie Emily Schofield')

- *Her downy cheeks stretched smooth and plump across wide cheekbones. Her eyes were deep and warm and brown …*

  (From 'Grandmother's Song')

Using these quotations, write a paragraph comparing the way the writers present older people. Think about the language techniques used and the impression each description creates of the grandmother.

> ### Reading tip
>
> When comparing information in texts, think about the best way to keep notes. Experiment with using spider diagrams, tables or bullet points until you find a method that suits you.

5 Most stories belong to a particular **genre** – a type of writing, such as adventure, comedy, crime, science fiction or romance. Different genres have different **conventions**. Conventions cover common 'rules' and ideas about how plot, characters and language are used.

'Grandmother's Song' belongs to the genre of folk tales. Look at this list of the conventions of folk tales. Which of these can you find in the story?

- a simple storyline containing repeated events
- simple words and phrases
- a journey
- a challenge or difficulty for the main character
- a simple setting (often unnamed)
- characters who are either good or bad
- themes about goodness, understanding and kindness
- a happy ending
- a lesson about life and/or human behaviour.

Folk tales

People choose books for many different reasons. For example, they may like the genre or have read and enjoyed books by the same author. Perhaps they read a good review of the book or liked the **blurb** on the back cover. Read the following descriptions of folk tales around the world.

> **Key words**
>
> **genre:** a particular type of text – for example, adventure, comedy, crime, science fiction
>
> **conventions:** the 'rules' of how a story is told or a piece of writing is set out

> **Key word**
>
> **blurb:** the information on the back cover of a book that tells the reader about the story

Princess Kwan-Yin – a Chinese folk tale

A king has three daughters, but his favourite is the youngest one, Kwan-Yin. He wants her to be queen when he gives up the throne. Kwan-Yin does not want to be queen – she thinks it will make her unhappy. She wants to spend her life studying and helping poor people. As the king is dying, he tells Kwan-Yin that he has found a husband for her and she must be married and become queen …

The Orphan Boy and the Mysterious Stone – a Nigerian folk tale

When his father and mother die, ten-year-old Ayong Kita becomes chief of the tribe. However, his people do not like him, so he runs away. He has no money and becomes very hungry, but has a dream in which his father tells him where to find buried treasure. He does not go because he is frightened. He then meets an old woman who gives him a stone from a lake. She tells him to go and dig up the treasure …

The Gold-Giving Snake – an Indian folk tale

At the end of a long day, a poor farmer called Haridatta falls asleep under a tree. He wakes up to find a giant snake coming out of its den. He decides to give it a bowl of milk, hoping that it will bring him good luck. The next day, he finds a gold coin in the bowl. Every time he gives the snake milk, it leaves him a gold coin. One day, Haridatta asks his son to feed the snake. His son decides to kill the snake and steal the gold from its den …

6 If you could only choose one of these stories to read in full, which would be your choice? Explain your choice to a partner and discuss your reasons.

Summary checklist

- [ ] I can summarise information from texts with similar themes, comparing and commenting on them.
- [ ] I understand the conventions of the folk tale genre.
- [ ] I can choose a story to read and give a reasoned explanation for my choice.

Check your progress

Answer the following questions.

1   Explain the ways in which writers establish setting at the start of a story.

2   Explain two ways that a writer can establish a character's voice.

3   Describe the different ways you could vary your voice when reading aloud.

4   Give an example of a story that contains aspects of cultural beliefs. Explain briefly how the story's cultural context affects its meaning.

5   What are the main themes in 'Grandmother's Song'?

6   Give three conventions of the folk tale genre.

Project

Every culture has its own folk tales. These stories are often spoken, but there are many examples of folk tales from around the world online and in published books.

In groups, you are going to read and then compile a short collection of folk tales. Each person in your group should choose a different country or continent. Then spend time individually researching and reading folk tales. Make brief notes on the titles and plots.

Once you have completed your research, each person in your group should choose one folk tale. Pick a tale that you think will interest the class, or one that says something distinctive about the culture it belongs to. Describe the tale to the group orally, then type it up. You could use pictures to suit the tale and edit the story if needed.

Once the group has collected the tales, create an **anthology** of all your tales. Then share them with the class. Enjoy reading and discussing them. Which ones did you like most of all and why?

Key word

anthology: a collection of poems or pieces of writing

3 Strange islands

In this unit, you will read about mysterious islands around the world. You will write and perform your own drama text, and read an adventure story set on an island.

> 3.1 The mystery of Oak Island

In this session, you will:

- identify and comment on implied meanings in a text
- interpret different language techniques
- explore the effects of informal language and non-standard English
- compare how characters are presented in non-fiction texts.

Getting started

Stories and real-life accounts of people discovering hidden objects and treasure are very popular. In pairs, discuss why these types of writing fascinate people. Have you ever found something interesting or valuable?

The Oak Island mystery

Read the following informative article about Oak Island in Canada.
The island is rumoured to contain hidden treasure.

Why are treasure hunters fascinated with this Canadian island?

Oak Island, a mysterious place in Nova Scotia, has long been an open secret in the world of treasure-hunting. Like a magnet, it has drawn many people to it over the years in hope of finding their fortune. The island first captured people's imagination almost 400 years ago. The initial rumour was that a dying sailor told an islander about a huge hoard of treasure buried there by Captain Kidd. Since then, the whole world has been intrigued by the island.

> hoard: a collection of valuable things, often kept hidden

In 1799, while Daniel McGinnis was looking for somewhere to build a farm on Oak Island, he found an area of land that seemed different to the rest. With two helpers, he dug into the ground and found a layer of stones placed less than 1 metre below the surface. As he dug further, he discovered wooden platforms and marks that looked like they'd been made by tools. But then, at about 9 metres down, the men experienced a strange feeling – a fear came over them and they stopped digging.

In 1909, the Old Gold Salvage Group arrived. They dug 34 metres down, but found nothing. In 1969, Triton Alliance bought most of the island and dug 72 metres down. They sent a camera into the hole and claimed to have recorded images of tools and wooden chests. People who saw the images said it was impossible to tell what was down there. Soon after that, the hole collapsed and the project was abandoned.

> Triton Alliance: an exploration group

As with many such mysteries, strange stories have emerged. Some people claim that the treasure included some unknown plays by William Shakespeare. Others say that a curse hangs over the island, which states that seven men will die before the treasure is found. So far, six men have died trying to find it …

In 2006, two brothers, Marty and Rick Lagina, bought half of the island. Since then they have found some items, including a coin and a sword, but nothing like the huge hoard of treasure supposedly buried there! The balance between what they have spent and what they have found seems very unequal.

1   Make notes on the different people who have searched for the treasure, according to the article. What did each group or person do and what did they find?

2   Explain what is implied by the final sentence: *The balance between what they have spent and what they have found seems very unequal.* What effect do you think the writer intended to have by ending in this way?

Reading tip

To work out what a writer is implying by a particular sentence, use clues from elsewhere in the text. Think about the writer's overall attitude to the topic – how does it fit with the sentence you are looking at?

3   Even in non-fiction writing, writers use language techniques to imply meaning. Copy and complete the table to suggest how each of the language devices from the first paragraph of the article could be interpreted. An example has been completed for you.

Example	Technique	Comment
an open secret in the world of treasure-hunting	**oxymoron**	
Like a magnet, it has drawn many people to it.	simile	
The island first captured people's imagination almost 400 years ago.	personification	This could be interpreted in two ways. Either the island is an attractive place, or it is a dangerous place that causes problems for treasure hunters – it traps them.
the whole world has been intrigued by the island	**hyperbole**	

Key words

oxymoron: a figure of speech that combines two contradictory ideas

hyperbole: exaggerated statements

Diggin' up the past

Now read another article about two Oak Island treasure hunters. This article is from a magazine written for young readers, containing entertaining accounts of people doing adventurous things. One of the ways it entertains the reader is by using language associated with the **stereotype** of a pirate.

Key word

stereotype: a familiar but simplified character type

The kool kidz diggin' for Kidd's treasure

Meet Marty and Ricky – Michigan's main men and coolest kids when it comes to findin' treasure! Together, these local heroes are unearthin' the secrets of Oak Island. As anyone from Michigan will tell you, these brothers are not only successful businessmen, they're also hunters – set on gettin' their paws on Cap'n Kidd's buried treasure. Cool!

As boys, they read about the mysterious Oak Island, off the coast of Nova Scotia in Canada – and they were hooked. They've spent their lives searchin' and even bought the island! Now that's dedication!

These boys have had to be careful, though – the island is a place of danger. Six people have died huntin' the treasure, but that ain't stopped our boys. With a team of experts, they've made some eye-poppingly amazin' finds. Their loot includes a mysterious Spanish coin, a strange metal cross and a Roman sword.

The famous Oak Island treasure is in their grasp – it's only a matter of time before they strike gold. And if anyone can do it, the Lagina brothers can. Go get 'em, boys!

4   Write a list of words and phrases that present the Lagina brothers in a positive way.

5   The tone of this article is informal. This comes across in the writer's choice of sentence types and punctuation, such as single-word sentences, dashes and exclamation marks. The writer also uses **non-standard English** word forms, such as dropping the final 'g', to sound more like a pirate.

Key words

non-standard English: words and grammatical patterns that fall outside the conventional forms of English

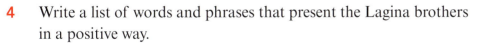

In pairs:

- Make a list of informal features in the article. Look for sentence and punctuation choices, contractions, words with the final letter missing and any deliberate misspellings.

- Discuss the effect of these choices. Does it make the article fun? Does it make the content of the article more or less believable?

6   The two articles present the Lagina brothers differently. Using the last paragraph from 'Why are treasure hunters fascinated with this Canadian island?' and the first paragraph from 'The kool kidz diggin' for Kidd's treasure', compare the way the brothers are presented. Write 150 words. You should comment on:

- the impression the writers give of the brothers

- the language the writers use.

Summary checklist

☐ I can work out implied meanings in a text.
☐ I can explain the meanings arising from the use of different literary techniques.
☐ I can comment on the effects of informal language and non-standard English.
☐ I can analyse how the same characters are presented in two different non-fiction texts.

> 3.2 Strange islands

In this session, you will:

- identify key information in audio and written texts
- explore how punctuation can be used to express formality and convey shades of meaning
- write and evaluate a descriptive piece.

How can different punctuation choices create different effects? In pairs, experiment with placing brackets, dashes and an exclamation mark to alter the tone of this sentence:

Although I've travelled to lots of places, including cities on all continents of the world, I was really excited to spend a month on a tiny island.

1 You are going to listen to an interview in which an expert explains how islands are formed. As you listen, make notes on the key points. Afterwards, use your notes to produce a poster displaying information about islands.

Unusual islands

Read this article, which describes some strange islands.

Listening tip

When listening to explanation texts, try to identify the different stages of the talk. For example, the introduction might often contain an overview, whereas key details are often found in the middle stages of a talk. You can use the structure of the talk to help you organise your notetaking.

Odd Islands Around the Globe

Most people think of islands as beautiful places where they can escape from the madness of life. However, while some islands are the perfect holiday destination, others are very unusual indeed …

Skorpios

Where? Greece

What's there? Skorpios is a place of sandy beaches, forests – and a helicopter landing pad! The super-rich Aristotle Onassis bought the island in 1963 and planted more than 200 different types of tree. It was once a place where exciting celebrity parties occurred. But by 2011, there were only five people living there. In 2018, however, a huge luxury resort was built on the island. Perhaps the fun will return!

Strangeness rating: 1/5 – Sounds like the perfect holiday!

Okunoshima

Where? Japan

What's there? Fancy a week among furry creatures? You're welcome to visit the Japanese island of Okunoshima, but you'd be wise to bring plenty of carrots – there are thousands of completely tame rabbits hopping around the place! The island, which is also known as Usaga Jima, used to be a chemical testing site. Many chemical weapons were used here (there's even a museum dedicated to poison gas on the island), but these days the rabbits are the main inhabitants.

Strangeness rating: 2/5 – Who's scared of rabbits?

Snake Island

Where? Brazil

What's there? If you dared to venture on to Snake Island, or Ilha da Queimada Grande to uses its proper name, you'd find yourself in the company of deadly snakes. Thousands of them. Snake Island has the largest number of snakes, mainly golden lancehead vipers, in such a small place. Although it was once home to humans (there was a lighthouse there until 1920), the island is now completely uninhabited. You really wouldn't want to visit – and in fact it's illegal to land on the island – but poachers have been known to secretly go there to catch and sell the snakes.

Strangeness rating: 4/5 – Dangerous and strange.

Island of the Dolls

Where? Mexico

What's there? On the Isla de las Munecas – Island of the Dolls – you'll find yourself faced with dolls. That's right … dolls. Or at least parts of dolls! Creepy, eh? The island can be found among the Xochimilco canals in Mexico City. It's thought that the man originally in charge of looking after the island – Don Julian Santana Barrera – found a floating doll and decided to build a collection. It was a long-term project for him. Over the next 50 years he put hundreds of dolls – or parts of dolls – around the island!

Strangeness rating: 5/5 – Seriously creepy.

2   Make notes in a table to summarise the main points about each island, the subsidiary information and any strange features.

Language focus

There are times when punctuation choices can help to create different effects. Punctuation such as brackets, dashes and exclamation marks are not only ways of organising information in a sentence, they also communicate levels of formality and different shades of meaning. Look at these examples and explanations.

- I went for a walk, even though it was getting late, and found myself lost in a maze of streets.

The commas give this a formal feel and a calm, explanatory tone.

- I went for a walk (even though it was getting late) and found myself lost in a maze of streets.

The brackets still give this statement a formal feel, but they create the impression of an aside – as if the narrator is involving the reader in their thoughts a little more.

- I went for a walk – even though it was getting late – and found myself lost in a maze of streets.

This example is less formal and more conversational. The dashes make it appear closer to spoken English, as if the narrator is casually (maybe quickly) explaining the situation.

- I went for a walk – even though it was getting late – and found myself lost in a maze of streets!

This example sounds more dramatic. The exclamation mark suggests heightened emotion, as if the narrator is scared or excited.

The choice of punctuation can help the reader to interpret the meaning of a sentence. Notice how the addition of the exclamation mark creates a different meaning to the version containing only commas.

---

3   In pairs, look at the range of punctuation in the description of 'Island of the Dolls'. How would you describe the overall effect of these features on the reader?

4   Write a 100-word description of Sable Island in Canada. Use the bulleted information on the next page to help you.

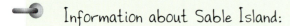

Your description should use the same style of structure, punctuation and language as the information in the article 'Odd Islands Around the Globe'.

Information about Sable Island:

- It belongs to Canada and is near Halifax.

- It experiences very strong winds.

- The extreme weather means that the landscape changes regularly.

- It is known as 'The Graveyard of the Atlantic' because of the number of wrecked ships near the island.

- Very few humans live there, but there are a lot of wild horses and one tree.

> **Writing tip**
>
> When asked to write in a particular format, start by identifying the structural features you will use, such as headings and subheadings. Count how many words are used in each section of the format and use this as a guide when drafting your text.

5 Swap your description with a partner. Read each other's description aloud. Focus on reading the text accurately and on using your voice to convey a lively tone.

Peer assessment

When you have listened to each other's readings, give your partner feedback.

- How accurately did your partner read your description?
- Did they use their voice to create a lively tone?
- Which parts were the most engaging to listen to? Why?

Summary checklist

☐ I can identify and make notes on the main points in texts I hear and read.

☐ I can understand how punctuation choices affect formality and can indicate shades of meaning.

☐ I can write and comment on a descriptive piece in a conversational tone.

> 3.3 *Treasure Island*: Meeting Ben Gunn

In this session, you will:

- work out the meaning of unfamiliar words in a text
- identify explicit information in a story
- explore the different ways a writer creates a character's voice
- write and evaluate a monologue.

Getting started

In pairs, write definitions of the words 'monologue' and 'contractions'. Check your definitions in a dictionary.

Treasure Island

Treasure Island by Robert Louis Stevenson was published in 1882. It tells the story of Jim Hawkins, a boy who finds himself sailing the seas looking for an island that is believed to contain buried treasure. His shipmates are old, strange pirates. They eventually find the island. Read the description of it.

Extract 1

Grey-coloured woods covered a large part of the surface. This even <u>tint</u> was indeed broken up by streaks of yellow sand-break in the lower lands, and by many tall trees of the pine family, <u>out-topping</u> the others – some <u>singly</u>, some in <u>clumps</u>; but the general colouring was uniform and sad. The hills ran up clear above the <u>vegetation</u> in spires of naked rock. All were strangely shaped, and the Spy-glass, which was by three or four hundred feet the tallest on the island, was likewise the strangest in <u>configuration</u>, running up <u>sheer</u> from almost every side and then suddenly cut off at the top like a <u>pedestal</u> to put a statue on.

1   When you read older texts, some words will be unfamiliar. Remind yourself of the strategies you used to work out unfamiliar words in Unit 1. Then use these to write down meanings of the underlined words in the extract. Check your definitions in a dictionary.

2   Using the description, draw a map showing the island's features. You will need to invent some details, such as the shape of the island.

Later in the story, Jim meets a pirate called Ben Gunn. Ben was there when another pirate, Captain Flint, buried treasure on the island.

Extract 2

'Who are you?' I asked.

'Ben Gunn,' he answered, and his voice sounded **hoarse** and awkward, like a rusty lock. 'I'm poor Ben Gunn, I am; and I haven't spoke with a person these three years.'

His skin, wherever it was exposed, was burnt by the sun; even his lips were black, and his fair eyes looked quite startling in so dark a face.

'Three years!' I cried. 'Were you shipwrecked?'

'Nay, mate,' said he; 'marooned.'

I had heard the word, and I knew it stood for a horrible kind of punishment common enough among the **buccaneers**, in which the offender is put ashore and left behind on some **desolate** and distant island.

I had made my mind up in a moment, and by way of answer told him the whole story of our voyage.

'You're a good lad, Jim,' he said; 'and you just put your trust in Ben Gunn.'

'Now, I'll tell you what,' he went on. 'So much I'll tell you, and no more. I were in Flint's ship when he buried the treasure; he and six strong seamen. They was ashore **nigh on** a week. Well, I was in another ship three years back, and we sighted this island. 'Boys,' said I, 'here's Flint's treasure; let's land and find it.' Twelve days they looked for it, and every day they had the worse word for me, until one fine morning all hands went aboard. 'As for you, Benjamin Gunn,' says they, 'here's a **musket**,' they says, 'and a spade, and pick-axe. You can stay here and find Flint's money for yourself,' they says.

Reading tip

When looking up a word in a dictionary, always check the different meanings and word class of the word. For example, the word 'beat' is both a noun and a verb. Make sure you identify the right meaning of the word in the context of the sentence.

---

hoarse: having a rough-sounding voice

buccaneers: sailors – often ones who were lawless

desolate: empty, uninhabited

nigh on: very nearly

musket: an old type of gun

3 Answer the following questions.

   a How long has it been since Ben met another person?

   b Describe Ben's appearance.

   c What does 'marooned' mean?

   d In your own words, describe how and why Ben was left on the island.

4 Look at the words and phrases in Ben's direct speech. The writer uses particular features to make the old pirate's voice interesting. In pairs, identify and discuss the effect of the following aspects of Ben's dialogue:

   • the way he refers to himself

   • non-standard English

   • the use of contractions.

5 Imagine you are Ben Gunn. Write a **monologue** as if you were talking to Jim. Tell him about how you spent your first day and night alone. Include details about:

   • how you felt

   • what you did for food and shelter

   • what you thought would happen in the weeks ahead.

Remember to use the same tone, language features and vocabulary as the writer uses for this character to capture Ben Gunn's voice.

6 Now read this sample monologue written by a learner. In pairs, discuss how effectively you think the response:

   • addresses the three bullet points in the task

   • captures Ben's voice.

> **Key word**
>
> **monologue:** a story or speech given by one character

I don't mind telling you, Jim, that first day was tough. Real tough. I'm not a pushover, Jim — nay — but I wept as I watched me shipmates sail away. Ben Gunn felt betrayed. I knew the treasure was here, but I couldn't find it, see? And when I saw how my shipmates looked at me, I knew no good could come of it. Their ship became a speck in the distance. And then it was gone. I sat on the sand and cried like a baby. I had a musket and some tools. That was it.

Islands is funny places, Jim. In daylight, they're beautiful, I tell you. At night, they're lonely and full of strange noises. I knew I needed shelter, so I headed inland. I spent the first day trying to find a safe place to sleep. At last Ben Gunn found a clump of bushes, small enough to sit inside. It has been my home for three long years now. I could make a fire and there was seawater. It makes you thirsty, Jim. There were berries to eat and strange fruit, but look at me — I'm thinner than a ship's cat.

The first night was cold and lonely. I never slept. Strange rustlings I could hear. There's sights and sounds on this island that would make the toughest pirate quake, Jim. When I woke up the next morning, a big cloud of sadness hung over me. The Cap'n had deserted me. I was alone and thought I'd die here. Nay — I knew I'd die here. If you could have seen me, Jim, you'd a said 'That Ben Gunn's a sad sight.' And you'd a been right.

Self-assessment

Reread your own monologue and think about how you could improve it.

- How well have you captured Ben's voice?
- Are spellings and punctuation accurate?

Summary checklist

- [ ] I can work out the meanings of unfamiliar words using a range of strategies.
- [ ] I can identify and comment on explicit meanings in a story.
- [ ] I can explain how tone, vocabulary and language features work to create a character's voice.
- [ ] I can write a monologue in the voice of a character, then evaluate and edit my work.

> 3.4 *Treasure Island*: The play

In this session, you will:

- stage a drama script
- explore how a drama script is written and structured
- write and perform a script based on a novel.

Getting started

How is a play script different to a novel? What are the 'rules' for setting out a script? What are stage directions? Discuss your thoughts with a partner and make some notes.

Speaking tip

Pauses are important when speaking. When performing a talk, use pauses to allow the audience time to take in what you have said. When reading a script, use pauses to help create tension or uncertainty.

1   Plays are often created from novels. They sometimes use dialogue from the original novel, but in many cases additional dialogue is needed. Scripts also need stage directions and guidance for actors on how to speak their lines. In groups of four, read this script aloud. It is a version of Jim and Ben's conversation. Decide who will take each of the following roles:

- Jim
- Ben
- sound-effects manager (who works out how to create the sound effects shown in the stage directions)
- director (responsible for advising Ben and Jim about their performance and checking their accuracy).

(An overgrown part of the island. Sound of footsteps and branches being hacked as JIM pushes and cuts his way through the trees and bushes.)

JIM: This place is … weird.

(JIM jumps in alarm as the loud sound of a colourful bird is heard.)

JIM: I need to get off this island. It's not normal.

(Sound of rustling. Someone is hiding.)

JIM: What's that? I can see eyes. Is that … a man? Hello!

(JIM'S 'hello' echoes around the island.)

BEN: Aaaargghhhh!

JIM: Aaaargghhhh!

(Both JIM and BEN are alarmed. Their screams echo loudly. Birds and other creatures scatter at the sound of their scream. The sound of wings beating and animals running is heard.)

BOTH: Who are you?!

BEN'S voice is rough. Both are scared. For a few seconds, they stare at each other.

JIM: I'm Jim Hawkins (*he says this loudly, attempting to sound brave*).

BEN: And I is Benjamin Gunn.

JIM: Are you … human?

BEN: (*laughs*) You cheeky young thing! Of course I is human! Have you ever seen a talking bear?

(Sound of musket fire in the distance.)

BEN: Are they here? Have they come back for me? Is that Captain Flint?

JIM: It's Long John Silver and his men. Do you know them?

BEN: I do, Jim. I do.

JIM: How long have you been here?

BEN: Three years (*his voice trembles*). Three long years. Three. Long. Years.

JIM: Why? How? Were you shipwrecked here?

BEN: Marooned, Jim. I was marooned.

JIM: (*questioningly*) Ma–what?

BEN: Marooned. Abandoned. Left behind. Me old mates left me here. It's a long story, Jim.

JIM: I think we've got time.

(Both laugh a little. Then the sound of musket fire, louder than before.)

BEN: Maybe not Jim. I'll be quick. I was in Flint's ship when he buried treasure somewhere on this island. I don't know where. He never let us see. But three years later, I came back here with another ship.

JIM: And what happened when you found the treasure?

BEN: We didn't. Twelve days we spent digging. In the end, they all turned on me.

(Pause.)

JIM: So they left you here as punishment?

> **BEN:** They did. Just me. And a musket. And a spade. And a pickaxe. 'Find Flint's money yourself' they yelled. So I watched their ship disappear and made a life here.
>
> *(Musket fire even louder.)*
>
> **JIM:** I need to get off this island.
>
> **BEN:** Me too. But I'm not leaving without the treasure.

2 In your groups, compare the script with the original story that you read in Session 3.3.

- What has been added? Do you think this is effective?

- How well do the stage directions allow you to picture the scene and characters?

- Are there any parts of the script that you feel do not work as well as the novel?

You are going to write a play version of another scene from *Treasure Island*. First, read this extract from the novel. Ben wants Jim to give a message to a man named Squire Livesey. Make notes to help you understand what is happening.

Extract 3

'Just you mention them words to your squire, Jim,' he went on. 'Nor he weren't, neither – that's the words.' And he pinched me again in the most confidential manner.

'Then,' he continued, 'then you'll say this: Gunn is a good man (you'll say), and he puts a precious sight more confidence in a gen'leman born than in these gen'leman of fortune.'

'Well,' I said, 'I don't understand one word that you've been saying. How am I to get on board?'

'If the worst come to the worst, we might try that after dark. Hi!' he broke out. 'What's that?'

For just then all the echoes of the island awoke and bellowed to the thunder of a cannon.

'They have begun to fight!' I cried. 'Follow me.'

And I began to run, my terrors all forgotten, while close at my side the marooned man trotted easily and lightly.

'Left, left,' says he; 'keep to your left hand, mate Jim! Under the trees with you!'

So he kept talking as I ran, neither expecting nor receiving any answer.

Language focus

Dialogue is the main way in which the story is told in a drama script. Sometimes, a character is given a long speech that reveals their feelings, but dialogue between characters is used to move the plot along and show cooperation or conflict. Playwrights use regular features in their dialogue, including:

- questions
- short sentences
- repeated phrases, questions and exclamations.

Writers also indicate in a script what tone of voice an actor should use to show how they are feeling. For example, these three versions of the same line suggest different things about the character's feelings:

- BETH: *(aggressively) Who's there?* – suggests she is angry or possibly afraid
- BETH: *(very quietly) Who's there?* – suggests she is calm or perhaps frightened
- BETH: *(annoyed) Who's there?* – suggests she is irritated.

3   Write a play script version of Extract 3. You should write 150 words. Use some dialogue from the extract, but remember to add more to make sure it is clear what is happening all the time. Use the layout of a script and the features of dialogue:

- set each speaker on a new line
- put the characters' names in the margin to show who is speaking
- use stage directions
- include questions, short sentences and exclamations.

- What were the main challenges when writing your script?
- How well did you solve these challenges?
- What will you do differently next time you write a script?

4   In groups, take turns performing each other's scripts. Remember
     to use your voices and gesture to convey the characters. Help each
     other to redraft lines where needed.

Summary checklist

- [ ] I can stage a drama script, using my voice to convey character and meaning.
- [ ] I can explain how a drama script is written and structured.
- [ ] I can write and perform a script based on an extract from a novel.

⟩ 3.5 Singing sand

In this session, you will:

- use clues to predict how a story might develop
- work out the meaning of unfamiliar words
- make notes on language and meaning in a story extract
- explore the effect of different sentence types and write compound-complex sentences.

Getting started

Stories often contain twists – unexpected developments in the middle or at the end of a story. What books have you read or films have you seen that contain surprising twists? Describe one of these plots to a partner. Try to explain why the twist was so effective. Think about what the writer or director had led you, as a reader or viewer, to believe. In your pairs discuss whether you like 'a twist in the tale' or if you prefer more predictable endings.

The Lost Island of Tamarind

You are going to read some extracts from a novel called *The Lost Island of Tamarind* by Nadia Aguiar. It tells the story of three children: Maya, her brother Simon and their baby sister, Penny. They have travelled to Tamarind to try to find their parents – Mami and Papi – who were last seen on the strange island. They have met a boy called Helix.

1   The title and genre of a story helps readers anticipate what it might be about. Establishing expectations is a key part of the reading process. In some stories, writers fulfil these expectations but in others they add unexpected twists to surprise their readers. *The Lost Island of Tamarind* is a story that contains elements of the **fantasy**, adventure and mystery genres.

Using all this information, write down some predictions about what will happen in the story and how it might end. Share your predictions in pairs.

2   Before you read the story, work out the meanings of the underlined words in pairs. Use a dictionary to check your answers.

Key word

fantasy: imaginative stories, often set in strange places with unusual characters

Extract 1

The children fell quiet. The jungle behind them and the sea before them were both <u>pitch-black</u> and when a cool breeze blew over them, they felt lost and lonely.

'I wish Mami were here,' said Simon softly.

Maya did, too. Her heart ached. A funny sound began to come from the edges of the darkness, from where the <u>palms</u> leaned over the beach and the shadows multiplied. A high, singing sound, like thousands of <u>delicate crystal chimes</u>, so beautiful it held the children transfixed. After a moment Maya noticed that the sand was shifting around them. A fine surface layer was rolling over itself. It was the <u>particles</u> of sand rubbing against one another that made the singing sound.

'Musical sand,' she whispered. 'Papi told me about it, that in some places in the world the sand sings.' Tears welled up in her eyes at the thought of her father.

Helix returned from bathing in the sea and suddenly Maya and Simon both felt more cheerful. He sat down by the fire. Penny was fast asleep already. <u>Lulled</u> by the singing sand, Simon was heavy-eyed and he yawned and <u>nestled</u> down in the sand, his head on his backpack.

Eventually the breeze died away, and the muggy breath of the jungle descended on to the beach. The sand lay silent in little <u>hillocks</u> of moonlight. Down by the shore, moonlight shone in the <u>tide pools</u>.

'Come and see the pools,' Helix said to Maya. 'We won't be far away – we'll be able to see your brother and sister the whole time.'

She nodded and they walked down to the tide pools.

3   Look at the details of the story and the way it has been written. Make notes on:

    a   the children's feelings (find quotations as evidence)

    b   details about the sights and sounds of the island

    c   any interesting language techniques used by the writer and their effects.

Now read the second part of the story.

Extract 2

The pools stretched out down the beach, and each one of them contained a reflection of the moon. Maya knelt down to look into one of the pools. As she watched, the reflection of the moon began to **recede** and a light inside the pool grew brighter and began to rise through the **shallows**, shattering the moon into dozens of soft, jagged pieces. It was some sort of sea creature that was casting the light, but it was still impossible to see the animal clearly beneath the rippling surface. Maya looked up and saw that other bright lights were surfacing in tide pools all the way down the beach.

When she looked back down at the tide pool, the surface of the water had settled and she could see the creature clearly. Her heart skipped a beat. A tiny, perfect octopus, just like the one that her parents had collected from the sea on their last day together,

> **recede:** go back, get smaller
>
> **shallows:** areas where the water is not very deep

was looking up at Maya. Its tentacles glowed so brightly that it outshone the moon. Then Maya realized that there were dozens of creatures just like it in the tide pools up and down the beach.

Was this where all the strange, glowing sea creatures that her parents had been collecting came from? Maybe it wasn't an accident that the children had landed in Tamarind. Could their parents have been looking for the island? Did these creatures have something to do with the Red Coral Project?

4   In these extracts, the writer varies sentence types for effect. For example, the simple sentence *Her heart ached* in Extract 1 describes Maya's feelings directly and shows the reader precisely how the character feels without adding unnecessary detail.

Look at the first paragraph of Extract 2. Write down one example each of a simple, a compound and a complex sentence and explain the effect of each sentence type. Think about what is happening in the story and how the sentence supports the actions and feelings created.

- How confident were you in identifying different sentence types?
- What methods did you use to identify them?

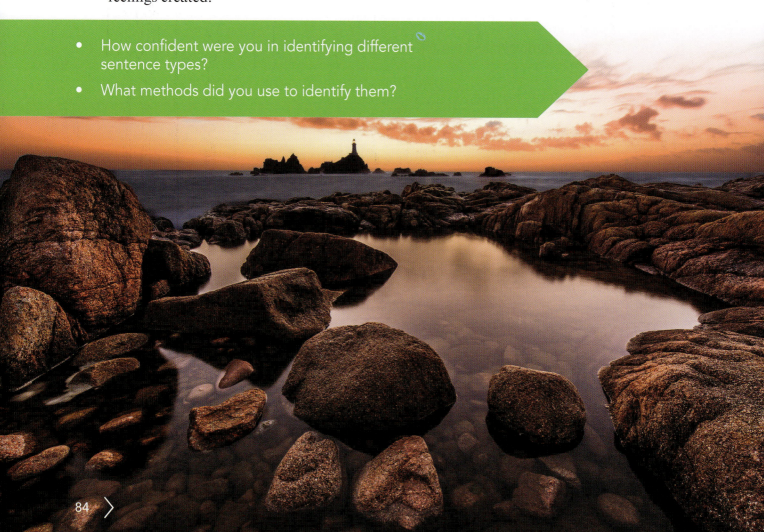

5 A compound-complex sentence contains two main clauses and a subordinate clause. For example:

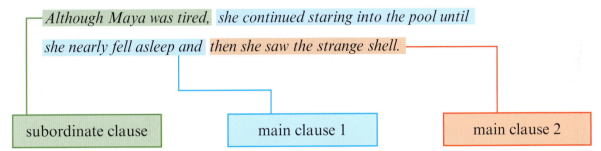

Although Maya was tired, *she continued staring into the pool until she nearly fell asleep and* *then she saw the strange shell.*

| subordinate clause | main clause 1 | main clause 2 |

Write a compound-complex sentence to describe Maya exploring the beach.

6 By the end of Extract 2, the reader has discovered several things, but there are also some mysteries.

- The children's parents are missing but we do not know how or why.
- The island has a strange atmosphere – the sand seems to cause Simon and Penny to sleep.
- It is not clear why Helix wants Maya to see the pools.
- The octopuses have an unusual glowing quality.
- Maya's parents have been collecting creatures but we do not know why.
- The Red Coral Project has been mentioned but not explained.

Using this information, work in pairs to predict how the story will develop.

> **Writing tip**
>
> When writing a compound-complex sentence, start by creating a compound sentence, then add the subordinate clause afterwards.

Summary checklist

- [ ] I can use genre clues to help predict how a story might develop.
- [ ] I can confidently work out the meaning of unfamiliar words.
- [ ] I can identify and analyse explicit and implicit meanings and language techniques in a story.
- [ ] I can comment on the effect of different sentence types and use compound-complex sentences.

› 3.6 Helix

In this session, you will:

- use different strategies to spell unfamiliar words
- consider how adverbs can add detail and meaning to sentences
- explore how writers present and develop characters
- respond imaginatively to a fictional character.

Getting started

What is an adverb? In pairs, come up with some examples of different types of adverb, then write some sentences using them.

Language focus

You can try several strategies when spelling unfamiliar or difficult words, such as:

- sounding out a word. This is where you say aloud the individual letters or syllables to help you hear each sound in the word.

- using your knowledge of root words and the patterns of words (morphology). For example, if you know how to spell 'identify' then you could work out how to spell 'unidentifiable'. You could do this by using your knowledge that adding the prefix 'un-' doesn't alter the start of the root word. Also, you could remember that when adding the suffix '-able' to words ending in '-y,' the last letter is dropped.

Most of the time, you will combine strategies. For example, if you needed to spell the word 'frustrated', then you could sound out the first five letters, then use your knowledge of other words using the suffix '-ed' to complete the word.

1   In pairs, help each other practise spelling using Session 3.5, Extract 2. One of you should choose five challenging words for your partner to spell. Then, you should swap roles and repeat the process with different words. Remember to use a range of strategies to help you spell the words accurately.

Now read the next part of *The Lost Island of Tamarind*. The first person to speak in this extract is Helix.

Extract 3

'I didn't want to tell you earlier,' he said. 'In front of your brother. But you may as well know, whether you take the river or come with me on foot, you aren't going to be able to find help in Port Town. Not the kind of help you're looking for. There's no one who can help you on Greater Tamarind.'

'What do you mean?' asked Maya. The good mood she had been in a moment before <u>abruptly</u> slipped away. 'Somebody has to be able to help us.'

'You don't know much about this place yet,' said Helix. 'But I know it isn't anything like where you came from. If I were you …' he said. He paused. 'If I were you, I'd try to start forgetting everything in your life before and get used to being here.'

'We're going to find our parents,' Maya said <u>coolly</u>.

'Well,' said Helix. 'You'll see.'

Maya didn't know what she had been thinking. Helix wasn't nice. The earlier mistrust she had felt for him flooded back. She looked at him <u>angrily</u>.

'What do you know?' she asked. 'You aren't much older than I am. Who are you to tell me we won't find our parents? And why are you out here by yourself, anyway?'

Helix didn't answer and Maya grew angrier.

2   One way in which writers build detail and convey feelings and attitudes is through their choice of **adverbs**. Look at the three adverbs underlined in the extract above. Each one reveals how Maya's attitude towards Helix has changed. Here are some sentences describing characters' speech and actions. For each sentence, suggest three adverbs that could fit into the gaps. Remember that most adverbs end in '-ly'.

a   'Get away from me!' shouted Amir _____.

b   'I'm frightened,' said Tim _____.

c   'I hope you will be back soon,' said Sisi _____.

> **Key word**
>
> adverb: a word that adds detail or information to a verb

3 Readers respond to characters in different ways and we often judge characters by what they say and do. A writer may want their readers to respond to characters differently at different points in a story. For example, a character who appears kind and thoughtful to begin with may later turn out to be the villain of the story.

How do you judge Helix and his actions? Look back at the three extracts from the story you have read so far. Note down what Helix says and does, and how he interacts with Maya. By the end of Extract 3, do you think he is a 'good' or 'bad' character? What clues can you find about how this character will develop? Find evidence from the text to support your ideas.

Now read the next part of *The Lost Island of Tamarind*.

Extract 4

'Oh, forget it,' she said, beginning to climb down the rocks, so quickly that she scraped her knees. She couldn't wait until she never had to see Helix again. 'I don't care what you say, anyway. We're going to find our parents, I'm going to make sure of it. And now I'm tired. Good *night.'*

Back with the others, Maya lay down in the sand so that Penny was sheltered between her and Simon. *Forget about Helix,* she thought. *Think about something else. Name the* **constellations**. She had memorized them, sitting wrapped in a blanket with her mother. Lying on the sand, Maya started with the constellations in the east and let her eyes travel west and read them across the sky as tiredness overtook her. Further down the beach the **glimmer** of the tide pools glowed on and she fell into a troubled sleep.

Later she thought she half woke, to see Helix sitting close to the fire for light, intently studying the pages of the **logbook**. She wanted to stop him – he had no right to be looking at their book – but sleep was too powerful and it pulled her back under before she could resist.

> **constellations:** a group of stars
> **glimmer:** to shine in a faint way
> **logbook:** a record of events on a ship

4   In this part of the story, Helix appears to take an unusual interest in the logbook, and we get the feeling that something is making Maya sleep against her will. Imagine you are Helix. Write an account from his point of view. In it, you should:

- tell the reader about yourself and how you came to the island

- give your thoughts about Maya and her search

- explain what you found in the logbook.

You will need to make up many of these details. Write 150 words.

Writing tip

When planning an imaginative account from a character's point of view, start by thinking about the character's **backstory**. This means imagining where they are from, what things they have done and their attitudes.

Key word

backstory: the fictional history or background created for a character in a story or film

---

Peer assessment

Swap your account with a partner and compare your writing:

- What choices have they made that are different to yours?

- Which parts of your partner's account do you like?

- Which parts do you think could be improved? Make suggestions.

Summary checklist

- [ ] I can use a range of different strategies to spell unfamiliar words.
- [ ] I understand how adverbs add detail and meaning to sentences.
- [ ] I can comment on how writers control their presentation of characters as a story develops.
- [ ] I can write from the viewpoint of a fictional character.

Check your progress

Answer these questions.

1   What is hyperbole? Give an example.

2   How do writers use language to create a conversational tone?

3   Write a summary of Ben Gunn's experiences in *Treasure Island*.

4   What are the rules for setting out a script?

5   'Genre clues can help readers predict how stories will develop'.
     Explain what this means.

6   Name and explain two strategies you could use to help spell unfamiliar words.

Project

In this unit, you have read about strange islands, both real and fictional. In groups, you are going to design your own island. You can decide where the island is in the world, what type of place it is and what happens there.

Start by choosing what atmosphere your island will have – it could be a quiet, strange island or an exciting, busy island filled with holidaymakers.

As you design your island, you could:

- think of a name for it

- design a map of it

- write brief accounts of the different places and creatures it is home to

- write a history of the island

- design a travel brochure for the island

- write a short story or play set there.

Once you have produced some of these materials, present them to the class. Think about how you will deliver the information. You could use drawings, a visual presentation or even perform a dramatic piece.

4 ▶ This is the modern world

In this unit, you will read about technological developments, discuss the impact of mobile phones and read fiction set in an alternative future.

❯ 4.1 The birth of the internet

In this session, you will:

- consider how structural choices help a reader
- analyse how language and punctuation are used to express formality
- compare the language and structure of two articles
- write an informative text for a specific audience.

Getting started

For certain types of texts and topics, it is important to consider your audience. In pairs, write two lists, noting down topics and text types where the age of the audience may or may not be important. Do you think that adults are only interested in more formal texts?

How it all happened

It is hard to imagine life before the internet, but have you ever wondered how and why it was developed? This article is from a magazine aimed at young people containing non-fiction, informative articles about a range of topics.

How the web was born

*It started as a way to keep secrets – now everyone knows about it! Want the word on the World Wide Web? Read on, **infophile**!*

Sputnik

The Cold War sounds like a **chilly** conflict, doesn't it? In reality, it was a time in the 1950s when the world might have been destroyed. The United States and the **Soviet Union** were not **seeing eye to eye**, and when the Soviets launched a satellite called Sputnik (crazy name, I know!) the Americans panicked. What would happen if US telephone lines were attacked from space? What could be done to protect communications from such an attack?

ARPAnet

The answer to the question was ARPAnet. In 1958, the Advanced Research Projects Agency was set up and by 1962, the ARPA network – or ARPAnet – had been created. Over the next ten years, developments resulted in data being passed between computers rather than over telephone wires. This was a significant moment in the birth of the internet.

NSFNET

In 1983, ARPAnet allowed the National Science Foundation Network (NSFNET) to use part of its network. This meant that networked communication was no longer just for military purposes. By 1985, engineers connected computers across IT departments in US universities.

infophile: someone who enjoys finding out information

chilly: a bit cold

Soviet Union: a group of countries that were under communist rule from the 1940s to the early 1990s

seeing eye to eye: on friendly terms

Tim becomes a parent

The World Wide Web as we know it was created in 1989. If it's right to talk about tech development as a birth, then Tim Berners-Lee was the daddy! His creation of hypertext transfer protocol – http to you and me – **sealed the deal**. By 1995, the internet was available to the public in their homes.

> **sealed the deal:** completed an agreement

We're not done yet …

It took almost 75 years to develop, but now more than three billion people use the internet. What will the next 75 years hold? Sit back and enjoy the ride …

Pushed for time? Here are the essentials:
- 1960s – ARPAnet invented to connect military computers
- 1980s – NSFNET connected university computers
- 1989 – Tim Berners-Lee created http and the internet was born.

1   Reread the article, making notes on the facts and key dates in the development of the internet. What did you learn that you did not know already?

2   The purpose of this article is to inform readers about the internet. In pairs, note down the structural features of the article. Bearing in mind the purpose of the article, how do these features help the reader?

3   The article addresses the reader in an informal way, but the writer also uses some formal language when giving technological information. Remember that voice and formality can be expressed through both language and punctuation choices.

Write a 150-word analysis of the effect these choices have on the reader. You could focus on:

- informal and formal language

- questions

- punctuation such as brackets, exclamation marks and ellipsis

- figurative language.

Reading tip

There is a subtle difference between the writer and the narrator of a text. The writer creates the whole text, including the voice, personality and attitude of the narrator. Writers adopt different voices and narrative personae to suit the audience and purpose they are writing for. Do not automatically assume that the writer's attitudes and views are the same as the voice narrating the text.

Tim Berners-Lee

This article is by the same writer, but it has a different audience. It was written for a website containing biographies of famous people. It is aimed at adults as well as young people. As you read, notice how the writer has chosen a different narrative voice to the one in the previous article.

Berners-Lee: a brief guide

Sir Tim Berners-Lee is best known for inventing the World Wide Web in 1989. He was educated at Oxford University, where he studied physics. In 1980, when working at the European Particle Physics Laboratory (known as CERN) in Switzerland, he proposed the concept of a global way of communicating known as hypertext. Four years later, he developed this concept by suggesting that hypertext and the internet could be joined together to share information around the world.

Sir Tim Berners-Lee has been given many awards for his work, including the Turing Prize for inventing the first web browser, the World Wide Web. He has also been awarded: the Millennium Technology Prize; the Japan Prize; the Die Quadriga award. In 2004, he was made a knight by Queen Elizabeth II of Great Britain, which gave him the title 'Sir'.

In recent years, Sir Tim has continued to develop projects connected with the internet. He is director of the World Wide Web Consortium, which manages the development of the web. He is Professor of Computer Science at Oxford University and the Massachusetts Institute of Technology (MIT). He appeared at the opening ceremony of the 2012 Olympics, where he tweeted the message 'This is for everyone'.

4 Compare the structure and language features of the two articles. Create a table to show the similarities and differences between:

- the way the articles are structured
- the formality of the language
- the use of punctuation.

How did these features affect your response to the topic?
Which of these texts was easier to read and follow? Why?

5 When writing an informative article, it is important to consider your audience. Ask yourself: who is your article aimed at? What tone and voice would be most appropriate?

Write an article aimed at people aged over 70, explaining how the internet was developed. Assume that your audience has some interest in computers but does not have the same knowledge that a younger person might have. Start by doing some research into the history of the internet. Collate and summarise information from a range of sources, then plan the structure and sequence of your work. Write 200 words.

Remember to:

- develop a clear voice in your writing
- use language and punctuation appropriate to the formality of your writing and the topic

- use clear handwriting
- use some of the strategies for spelling correctly that you learnt in Session 3.6.

Peer assessment

Swap your writing with a partner and consider the choices they have made.

- Are voice and level of formality suitable for the audience? Why or why not?
- Have they clearly explained the information? How could it be made clearer?
- What advice could you give to improve the structure?

Summary checklist

- ☐ I understand how writers make structural choices to help a reader's understanding.
- ☐ I can analyse the use of language and punctuation to express levels of formality.
- ☐ I can identify and compare structural and language features in two texts.
- ☐ I can research and write an informative article for a particular audience.

Writing tip

When you write for different audiences, think carefully about the topic and consider what your intended reader is likely to know already. What information will be most useful to them? What is the best way to structure your writing to make this information clear?

> 4.2 Phone problems

In this session, you will:

- discuss the meaning and effect of variations when communicating
- consider the impact of bias in a text
- compare viewpoints in several texts
- plan and deliver a persuasive speech.

People vary the way they speak in different situations. In pairs, come up with some different everyday situations and discuss how you speak in each one. What factors influence the changes in the way you speak? For example, consider how you talk to:

- your parents
- a sibling (a brother or sister)
- your best friend
- the local shopkeeper
- your teacher.

1 Mobile phones can be extremely useful, but some people believe that they are a negative influence on people's lives. Listen to Anika talk about phones. In the first half, she is discussing them with her friend, Sahana, at home. In the second, she is talking to her teacher, Mrs Chana, in a lesson.

    a Make notes on the way Anika varies how she communicates in each discussion. Think about the words she uses, her tone and the level of formality.

    b In pairs, discuss what these variations suggest and what impact they have on the listener.

Two views

Persuasive texts offer strong opinions supported by reasons and justifications. They are meant to persuade the reader that the opinion they contain is valid. However, persuasive texts may present a **biased** view.

Read the two extracts on the next page, which are about mobile phones and young people. The first view is from Samir, whose daughter recently left school. The second is by Liu, chief executive of a leading media company. Both texts are written to persuade readers to agree with their way of thinking. As you read, think carefully about who is speaking and how they present their ideas.

Samir

Fellow parents, think very carefully about your children's relationship with technology. I let my daughter have a phone when she was 13 and it was a disaster. Our relationship changed. She stopped talking and became almost a stranger. She stopped going out and spent hours staring at her phone, messaging friends and watching silly videos. When I suggested to her that she shouldn't use her phone so much, she got angry and said that all her friends used their phones just as much as she did. The problem, according to my daughter, was me – not the phone. So I did what any parent would do and banned her from using it. After a few months, she was back on it. I gave up. The result was that she did badly in her exams. My message to parents is that phones take over children's lives, and once they do, there's no going back. Don't let your child have a phone or you'll regret it.

Liu

To any parents reading this who are wondering whether to let their children have a phone, I'd say don't hesitate. The arrival of phones has changed children's lives for the better. Today's young people are smart, aware and free to interact with the world. Can you remember what it was like in the age before we had mobile technology? I can and let me tell you, it was dull! My own children know much more than I did when I was at their age. They are never bored and they are doing far better at school than ever before. Anyone who thinks that they can stop children from using modern technology is wasting their time. Mobile technology is here and our children deserve the right to access it.

2 Reread the two views. Work in pairs.

  a Summarise the main points made by each speaker.

  b Discuss the impact of these views. How do you respond to the ideas in each text? Were you persuaded by their points?

Growing up in the modern world

The following **blog** is written by a mother about her daughter, Kylie. In it, she explores her daughter's use of her phone. Its purpose is to discuss the topic, rather than to persuade. Discussion texts consider different opinions in a measured way. They usually conclude with the writer's overall view.

Blog	About	Home	🔍

When Kylie was six, she was such a creative kid. Somewhere along the line though, creative play was replaced with video games, and drawing became social media. Now she is a teenager, Kylie still plays, but the games she plays are not in the family home, they're somewhere in the digital world. It's a world I'm no longer required to be part of: the screen of her phone is also out of my reach, often tilted away from my view and hidden behind a passcode. I'm still not sure what I think about children, parents and privacy.

Everyone thinks their childhood was better than their own kids'. Less technologically advanced, but more innocent. Outdoors rather than indoors. Yet when I really think about it, I reckon the children of this generation have got much to celebrate. Technology has made them communicate, just in a different way. Social media is primarily about feelings. And Kylie is fantastic at reading people. She knows how to challenge, comfort and entertain.

My daughter's digital teen years are mainly good ones. On her phone, she can find a recipe for the family meals she makes, she has learnt how to speak two different languages and she gets involved with the issues I want her to know about: global poverty, justice and equality. Most importantly, her childhood has taught her how to understand people. Kylie cares. She cares for people, animals and anything that exists. I'm not honestly sure whether the modern world with its technology is always a good thing, but at its best, it's a force for good.

3 Reread the blog.

a Make notes on the writer's views as they develop.

b Compare the views expressed to those of Samir and Liu from Activity 2. Which view do you agree with most and why? Explore your thoughts in pairs.

4 Many schools do not allow learners to use their phones or other mobile technology. Imagine you attend a school that is debating whether or not to let learners use phones and tablets in the classroom to help with learning.

Prepare and deliver a speech persuading your school to use mobile technology in class. You can use some of the information from this session, along with your own ideas. Your speech should last one minute.

Start by planning the points you will make and the order you will use them in your speech. You could also use common techniques found in persuasive texts, such as:

- hyperbole
- **rhetorical questions**
- exclamations
- statistics
- **triples**
- **emotive language**
- repetition
- figurative language
- **direct address**
- **imperatives**.

When you deliver your speech, think about how you could use gesture and other non-verbal actions. Decide whether to use notes or visual aids during your speech.

> ### Speaking tip
>
> Remember that the content of a persuasive speech is more important than the language techniques you use. People are persuaded by ideas and emotions rather than techniques, so make sure that your points are clear and convincing.

> ### Key words
>
> **rhetorical questions:** questions designed to make a point rather than expecting an answer
>
> **triples:** three words used together in a list for persuasive effect
>
> **emotive language:** language designed to appeal to a reader's emotions

> ### Key words
>
> **direct address:** speaking directly to any audience using pronouns such as 'you'
>
> **imperative:** a word or phrase styled as an order or command

- How confident did you feel when delivering your speech?
- What would you change or develop next time you give a speech?

Summary checklist

☐ I can identify how, why and to what effect people vary their speech in different situations.

☐ I can comment on the impact of bias in a text.

☐ I can compare the viewpoints expressed in different texts on similar themes.

☐ I can research, plan and deliver a persuasive speech, using a range of persuasive techniques.

> 4.3 Predicting the future

In this session, you will:

- have a group discussion in response to a text
- explore the techniques writers use to establish voice
- write in an entertaining voice
- express and justify a response to a text.

Getting started

Think of some entertaining writing you have read. What did you enjoy about it? What techniques did the writer use to make the text fun and interesting? In pairs, discuss how writers create entertaining stories and articles.

Looking to the future

Read this article from a website that contains light-hearted stories and articles. It is an account of predictions from the past – things that people thought would happen by 2020.

The future is here!

Ever wondered what might happen in the future? Flying cars? Computers in brains? Although the world has changed dramatically in the past 50 years, we haven't quite reached the stage where teachers are made from metal. Yet. In the past, though, people had some crazy ideas about what the year 2020 would be like. But just how accurate were they? Read on …

No work

Sounds good to me! In the 1960s, an article in the magazine *Time* claimed that by 2020, everybody would be very rich indeed. The idea was that instead of working ourselves to exhaustion (which let's face it, we all do), machines would do all the work. Humans would do nothing except count the money. Imagine the fun you could have …

Accuracy score: 0 out of 10. I'm still working.

No food

This isn't quite as bad as it sounds – to be honest, it sounds awful – but it actually wasn't a scary belief that there'd be nothing to eat in the future. No, this is the strange prediction made by Ray Kurzweil in a 2005 book. He claimed that by 2020, humans wouldn't need food. Instead, technology would feed our bodies and remove waste products. The result – no need to eat. How boring would that be?

Accuracy score: 0 out of 10. I'm still cooking.

Flying houses

This next prediction is about … well, flying houses, as you may have guessed from the subheading! In the 1960s, Arthur C. Clarke, a leading writer and inventor, reckoned that by 2020, we'd have houses that could move to other streets, towns and even countries. Could be fun – if it gets too hot in Mumbai, you could always fly to Iceland!

Accuracy score: 0 out of 10. I'm still on the ground.

So, a big fat zero for all of those predictions. Shame. But were there any predictions that did come true? Well, Arthur C. Clarke wrote about an electronic device that stored lots of information for humans to read. He called it a Newspad. Sounds familiar …

1 In groups, discuss each of the predictions. Which one do you wish had come true and why? Remember to take turns expressing your views and listen carefully to other people's ideas.

Language focus

Placing different sentence types alongside each other not only makes a text more interesting to read, it also helps to create different tones and voices.

Look at this example:

- I lay in bed and listened with horror to the strange sound that echoed from the staircase. Creak, it went. I'd never been so scared in my life.

Tension is created by placing a short, simple sentence ('Creak, it went') at the moment of drama in the story. Its effect is heightened by the contrast with the more descriptive compound-complex sentence that comes before it. In the context of the paragraph, it helps to create the voice – that of a tense, worried narrator.

Now look at another example:

- I looked at the students in my class with my most severe look, which admittedly I didn't use too often, and demanded to know why they weren't taking me seriously. Then it dawned on me. I was wearing odd shoes.

Here, the writer creates **humour** by placing two simple sentences at the end of the account. The shortness of the sentences suggests the narrator's embarrassment. Again, they are made effective by the preceding compound-complex sentence. In the context of the paragraph, it helps to create the voice – that of the embarrassed and knowingly comic narrator.

> **Key word**
>
> humour: when things are funny, or things that are comical

2   The voice of a text reflects its topic, purpose and audience. For example, a text written to entertain an audience about a humorous topic might be written in a light-hearted, informal voice. A persuasive article about a serious topic will use a serious, formal voice. Voice is shown in the content – what is being written about – but language, punctuation and sentence choices also help to establish voice.

The future is here! is written in an entertaining voice. Make notes on the different ways that the writer establishes this voice. Consider the choice of vocabulary, punctuation and the placement of different sentence types next to each other.

3   What strange and unusual things do you think might happen in the future? Write a prediction explaining how technology might change our lives by 2050. Write 100 words using an entertaining voice. Choose vocabulary and punctuation carefully. Try to vary your sentence structures for effect – think about the placement of different types of sentence.

> ### Writing tip
>
> When writing to entertain or create humour, it can help to think of a specific reader – such as a friend or family member – and focus on them as you write. Consider what would entertain that particular person and use that as inspiration.

> ### Peer assessment
>
> Swap predictions with a partner.
> - What do you think of their prediction?
> - What interesting vocabulary, punctuation and sentence structures have they used?
> - What was the effect of these choices?

Humans versus Machines

Now read 'Rise of the Machines' – a more serious view of technology and the future.

Rise of the Machines

The future is usually filled with hope: most people think it will be a better place where life will be happier, easier and longer. I used to think this, but the rise of the machines – by which I mean the way computers have taken over our lives – fills me with anxiety.

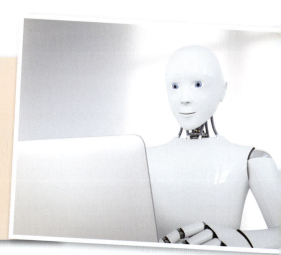

It's a fact that over the years, computers have replaced humans. The jobs that humans used to do are now being done by machines. We're being replaced by robots. Now.

Look at the way people have become dependent on technology in their daily lives: a simple example is how we have come to rely on maps on our phones instead of using our brains. It's making us lazy. Lazy and irrelevant. At some point, we might even stop talking to each other and just let computers do it.

Where will it end? What happens if computers and **artificial intelligence** take over? What happens when we become the slaves and they become the masters? I'd try to persuade you to take a stand against the rise of the machines, but I fear it is too late. The future is here already.

> **artificial intelligence:** machines such as computers and robots that have human-like intelligence

4   Make notes on the voice of the text, considering the use of vocabulary, punctuation and sentence structures.
    Then in pairs, discuss:

    • what type of text this is – what is its purpose?

    • which choices of vocabulary, punctuation and sentence structures were particularly effective?

5   Here are two views about this article. Which view do you agree with most and why? Discuss your ideas in pairs. Make sure you justify your view.

This is an accurate account of how technology has taken over. I think that human life is gradually being changed for the worse because of the way we rely on technology.

This is a very negative account of the influence of technology. The writer exaggerates the effects of computers on humanity and sounds a bit silly.

Summary checklist

- ☐ I can participate in a group discussion, listening carefully and contribute my own ideas.
- ☐ I can explain some of the techniques writers use when creating different voices.
- ☐ I can write in an entertaining voice.
- ☐ I can express a personal response to a text and justify my opinion.

> 4.4 A dystopian future

In this session, you will:

- explore the features of dystopian fiction genre
- express a personal response to some texts
- consider how context can inform the writing and reading of a story
- plan and write a story summary.

Getting started

A dystopia is a world where things have changed for the worse. What books and films can you think of that are set in a terrible future world? What sorts of things happen in these books and films? Discuss your ideas in small groups.

1   These summaries describe part of the plot of two dystopian stories. As you read them, make notes on:

- the type of characters the stories feature
- what happens in the plots
- what you notice about the settings.

The Queue

This book by Basma Abdel Aziz tells the story of Yehya, a man from an unnamed city in the Middle East. Yehya has been injured in a mysterious confrontation called the Disgraceful Events. He needs to have a bullet removed from his body, but it is illegal for a doctor to do it without a **permit**. The only way to get a permit is to go to the Gate and join the Queue. There are lots of people in the Queue who are trying to get permits for medical treatment. The Queue never moves – it just gets longer. Meanwhile, a strange media company is giving away free phones, all newspapers have been replaced by one called *The Truth*, and a journalist is trying to find out what is going on.

permit: a licence that grants permission to do something

Leila

This story by Prayaag Akbar is set in the late 2040s and features the characters Shalini and Riz. They have a three-year-old daughter called Leila. In the city where they live, different groups have built walls to keep themselves apart from others because the city council has promoted the idea of 'Purity for All'. Some **sectors** are rich and some very poor. Travel between sectors is discouraged and controlled by a violent gang called Repeaters. Shalini and Riz are from two different communities; they live in an area on the edge of the city rather than in one of the sectors. A gang of Repeaters arrives at Leila's birthday party, attacks Riz and sends Shalini to a Purity Camp. Leila and Sapna (her nanny) manage to escape.

sector: an area or part of the city

2 Which of these stories sounds most interesting to you?
Justify your choice to a partner.

- How easy was it to justify your choice?
- What makes you choose one book or type of story over another?

Dystopian fiction

Some stories are popular within certain cultures and countries. This could be because they reflect the values of the country in which they are written and celebrate aspects of that culture. People often enjoy dystopian fiction because they believe it says something important about humans. Read this text, which analyses why dystopian fiction is popular.

Why we love terrible stories

It seems that misery is popular. Readers can't get enough of dystopian fiction – stories set in a terrible future in which nice people experience awful things. I asked leading publisher Laika Masood why dystopian fiction sold well. 'It's probably because it deals with human fears,' she said. 'At some level, most people fear being controlled by those more powerful than them, or having their identities and personalities squashed, and dystopian fiction explores that in an extreme way.'

It's also true that dystopian fiction reflects something about the time in which it is written. Laika explained that 'the genre sells well when society is a bit depressed or people feel that their world is changing'. So do people only read this type of book when they're feeling unhappy? Probably not. People read for all sorts of reasons, but it is the case that when and where you read a text affects how you respond. In other words, if you live a peaceful, content life then you may react differently than if you live in a place which is heavily controlled.

3 Explain what the writer means by the following statements:

a *it deals with human fears*

b *dystopian fiction reflects something about the time in which it is written*

c *when and where you read a text affects how you respond.*

4   The publisher has asked you to write a dystopian novel. Before you do this, they need you to summarise the characters, setting and some of the plot. This means writing a summary like those in Activity 1. This is your basic idea:

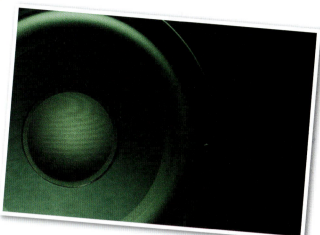

A national company has been giving away free speakers to every home in the country. People don't realise that these devices can listen in on conversations.

Create a plan that includes some more plot details, a setting and one or two key characters. Decide how to generate and record your ideas before creating your plan.

Writing tip

When planning a story, it is useful to start by mapping out the basic plot on a horizontal line. This will help you to work out the order and to see how the various events in the story structure relate to each other.

Language focus

There are times in writing when it is important to use clear, direct language rather than to write in a complex way. This means choosing words and sentence structures that get a point across clearly. For example, compare these two sentences about the same story:

- In this novel, which is the type of tale that may appeal to a host of dystopian fiction lovers, the narrative centres on two distinct character types: one is Shay, who is an attractive but deeply complex persona, and the other is Magenta, a girl who (despite leaving school with few qualifications) exhibits the sort of qualities that mark her out as a deeply intellectual character.

- This story is about two characters: Shay, a complicated boy and Magenta, an intelligent girl.

Notice how the second example uses clearer language and simpler sentence structures. It also does not include unnecessary information about genre and specific character details.

5   Now write your own summary. Use clear, direct language. You are summarising here, rather than providing lots of detail in complex words, so use the examples at the start of this session as models. Write 150 words.

Summary checklist

- [ ] I can describe some features of dystopian fiction, including character, setting and plot.
- [ ] I can express preferences and justify my choices.
- [ ] I can explain how the context of a story might inform how it is both written and read.
- [ ] I can plan and write a story summary.

> 4.5 The Glade

In this session, you will:

- explore how a writer creates an effective setting
- use language techniques to establish setting and mood
- create emotional effect in writing through word choices.

Getting started

Think of some distinctive settings in stories you have read. What makes them memorable? Discuss your ideas in pairs.

The Maze Runner

The Maze Runner by James Dashner is about a boy called Thomas who finds himself in a place called the Glade. He has no memory of how he got there. The Glade is surrounded by high walls, with openings

that shut every night. Beyond the walls is an area known as The Maze.
As you read, use a range of strategies to work out any words that are
unfamiliar to you.

Extract 1

Thomas leaned against the tree as he waited for Chuck.
He scanned the compound of the Glade, this new place of
nightmares where he seemed destined to live. The shadows from
the walls had lengthened considerably, already **creeping** up the
sides of the ivy-covered stone faces of the other side.

At least this helped Thomas know directions – the wooden
building crouched in the northwest corner, the grove of trees
in the southwest. The farm area, where a few workers were
still picking their way through the fields, spread across the
entire northeast quarter of the Glade. The animals were in
the southeast corner, mooing and crowing
and **baying**.

In the exact middle of the courtyard, the hole
of the Box lay open, as if inviting him to jump
back in and go home. Near that, maybe six
metres to the south, stood a squat building
made of rough concrete blocks, a menacing
iron door its only entrance – there were no
windows. A large round handle **resembling**
a steel steering wheel marked the only way
to open the door, just like something within
a submarine. Despite what he'd just seen,
Thomas didn't know what he felt more
strongly – curiosity to know what was inside,
or **dread** at finding out.

> **creeping:** moving slowly
> **baying:** howling
> **resembling:** looking like
> **dread:** great fear

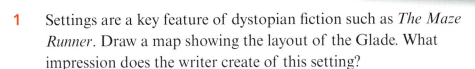

1   Settings are a key feature of dystopian fiction such as *The Maze
    Runner*. Draw a map showing the layout of the Glade. What
    impression does the writer create of this setting?

2   The writer uses various techniques to describe the setting in
    the extract. For example, he uses personification in the phrase
    the wooden building crouched. This makes the building seem
    unattractive and as if it does not want to be there and suggests the
    uncomfortable nature of the setting.

What overall effect do these examples of personification and aural imagery create?

a   *The shadows from the walls … creeping up the sides of the ivy-covered stone faces of the other side.*

b   *The animals were … mooing and crowing and baying.*

c   *a menacing iron door its only entrance*

3   Write a description of your own dystopian setting. It could be based on the novel you planned in Session 4.4, or you can think of a new one. Use vocabulary and language techniques to reflect the setting clearly and to create an unsettling mood. Write 200 words.

Writing tip

Remember, you can change and improve word choices when you redraft your writing. Use a thesaurus to help you find and use words with different shades of meaning. However, try not to use too many unusual words, as this can make your writing seem forced rather than natural.

Now read the next extract from the novel where Chuck shows Thomas around the Glade.

Extract 2

They reached the <u>huge</u> split that led outside to more stone pathways.

'This is called the East Door,' Chuck said, as if proudly <u>revealing</u> a piece of art he'd created.

Thomas barely heard him, <u>shocked</u> by how much <u>bigger</u> it was up close. At least six metres across, the breaks in the wall went all the way to the top, far above. The edges were smooth, except for one odd, repeating pattern on both sides. On the left side of the East Door, <u>deep</u> holes several centimetres in diameter and spaced thirty centimetres apart were bored into the rock, <u>beginning</u> near the ground and continuing all the way up.

On the right side of the Door, rods thirty centimetres long and ten in diameter **jutted out** from the wall edge, in the same pattern as the holes facing them on the other side. The purpose was obvious.

'Are you **kidding**?' Thomas asked, the dread slamming back into his **gut**. 'You weren't playing with me? The walls really *move*?'

'What else would I have meant?'

How could these walls move? They're huge, and they look like they've been standing here for a thousand years. And the idea of those walls closing and trapping him inside this place they called the Glade was terrifying.

> **jutted out:** stuck out
> **kidding:** joking
> **gut:** stomach

Language focus

English has a range of alternative words, or **synonyms**, with different shades of meaning. In creative writing, it is important to select the word that best conveys the meaning and atmosphere you want to create. For example, look at these two sentences that describe a boy looking at the sky:

- He saw the sky; it looked sad.

- He peered at the sky; it looked sombre.

The first example uses the common single-**syllable** words *saw* and *sad* and its simplicity clearly expresses the situation. The second example uses more complex words. This version gives more detail about the way the boy is looking ('peered').

Appropriate word choices depend on many things, including audience and purpose. In an adventure story for young children, the word 'sombre' seems too complex, but it is an appropriate description in a story for older readers. Even in writing for older readers, there may be times when simple, direct language is more suitable. For example, simple language can help create a sense of urgency and excitement. It is also useful for clarity when you want the reader to quickly understand what is happening, when complex vocabulary might interrupt the flow of the text.

Key words

synonym: a word or phrase with the same or similar meaning to another word or phrase

syllable: a word or part of a word that has one vowel sound

4   In this extract, the writer uses straightforward words for effect, rather than richly descriptive language. In pairs, note down some more complex alternatives for the underlined words in the text. Discuss the different effect created. Do you agree that more complex word choices would be unhelpful at this point in the story?

5   The language choices in this part of the story become more vivid as Thomas realises the situation he is in. For example, phrases such as *dread slamming back into his gut* and *the Glade was terrifying* suggest aggressive, frightening feelings and create a dramatic emotional effect.

Write a paragraph that includes dramatic words and phrases like the examples above, to create a sense of tension. Use this picture as a starting point.

Peer assessment

Swap paragraphs with a partner.

- Which words and phrases in their writing create the sense of tension?
- What can you suggest to help your partner improve their writing?

Summary checklist

☐ I can comment on the impact of language used to describe a setting.

☐ I can use vocabulary precisely to establish a setting and mood.

☐ I can choose words to create an emotional effect in a dramatic paragraph.

〉 4.6 Closing doors

In this session, you will:

- consider when, how and why writers withhold and reveal information
- explore how structural and language features can be combined for effect
- analyse the climax of a narrative
- write a climactic scene with an atmosphere of terror.

Getting started

In pairs, discuss what is meant by 'tension' in and the 'climax' of a story? Make a list of stories you have read that contain these features. How do you feel when reading stories that use tension to build to a climax?

Read the next extract from *The Maze Runner*.

Extract 3

His heart skipped a beat when a boy unexpectedly appeared around a corner up ahead, entering the main passage from the right, running towards him and the Glade. Covered in sweat, his face red, clothes sticking to his body, the boy didn't slow, hardly glancing at Thomas as he went past. He headed straight for the squat concrete buildings located near the box.

Thomas turned as he passed, his eyes **riveted** to the exhausted runner, unsure why this new development surprised him so much. Why *wouldn't* people go out and search the maze? Then he realised others were entering through the remaining three Glade openings, all of them running and looking as ragged as the guy who'd just whisked by him. There couldn't be much good about the maze if these guys came back looking so **weary** and worn.

He watched, curious, as they met at the big iron door of the small building; one of the boys turned the rusty wheel handle,

> **riveted:** looking intently at
> **weary:** very tired

grunting with the effort. Chuck had said something about runners earlier. What had they been doing out there?

The big door finally popped open, and with a deafening squeal of metal against metal, the boys swung it wide. They disappeared inside, pulling it shut behind them. Thomas stared, his mind churning to come up with any possible explanation for what he'd just witnessed. Nothing developed, but something about that creepy old building gave him goose bumps, a disquieting **chill**.

chill: a feeling of fear

1 One of the key structural decisions a fiction writer makes is how much information to reveal to the reader. What level of knowledge they decide to share often depends on the effect they hope to create. Withholding information can create effects such as a release of tension or tension or mystery. Revealing information may create sudden humour. Make notes on:

- what the reader and Thomas *don't* know – what mysteries are there?

- the effect this lack of knowledge has on the reader and Thomas.

Reading tip

When considering the level of knowledge the reader has, look at how the writer gradually reveals information as the story progresses. Explore any new information in each paragraph and identify the point in the structure when crucial information is revealed.

- How easy did you find it to comment on the way a writer controls the reader's knowledge?

- What advice would you give to another learner on how to develop this skill?

2   In Extract 3, the writer also uses sensory images to create particular effects. For example, in the first paragraph, tactile images such as *Covered in sweat, his face red, clothes sticking to his body, the boy didn't slow* reveal the physical exertion the boy has experienced. They make the reader and Thomas wonder just what is happening. Aural images also create a sense of mystery. For example, the sounds described in the third paragraph make the reader wonder why so much effort is being put into opening the door.

Reread the final paragraph of the extract. Write 100 words explaining how the writer combines structural and image choices and the effect that this creates.

Now read the next part of the story.

Extract 4

Before Thomas had a chance to think, questions were rushing out of his mouth. 'Who are those guys and what were they doing? What's in that building?' He wheeled around and pointed out the East Door. 'And why do you live inside a maze?' He felt a rattling pressure of uncertainty, making his head splinter with pain.

'I'm not saying another word,' Chuck replied. He stopped, held up a finger, pricking up his right ear – 'it's about to happen.'

A loud boom exploded through the air, making Thomas jump. It was followed by a horrible crunching, grinding sound. He **stumbled** backwards, fell to the ground. It felt as if the whole earth shook; he looked around, panicked. The walls were closing. The walls were *really* closing – trapping him inside the Glade. A sense of **claustrophobia** stifled him, **compressing** his lungs, as if water filled their cavities.

He looked around at the other openings. It felt like his head was **spinning** faster than his body, and his stomach flipped over with dizziness. On all four sides of the Glade, only the right walls were moving, towards the left, closing the gap of the Doors.

stumbled: trip, almost fall

claustrophobia: fear of small spaces

compressing: squeezing

spinning: rotating

3   List five sentences from this extract you feel are most effective in creating an emotional impact. Compare your lists in pairs.

4   This extract marks part of the **climax** in the **narrative**. How does the writer show Thomas's terror here? Consider both structural and language choices. Write 150 words, including relevant quotations to support your points. You could include:

- the use of questions in dialogue

- different types of images

- verb and adjective choices

- the focus on Thomas's reactions.

5   Using the extract as a model, write a climactic scene in which you create a sense of terror. Write 150 words. Develop the scene from one of these ideas:

- a girl trapped in a series of endless corridors

- a boy lost in a cave which begins to fill with water.

Key words

climax: the most exciting or important part of something

narrative: a series of connected events that are written or spoken

Summary checklist

☐ I can explain how and why a writer withholds or reveals information to a reader.

☐ I can describe the effects of structural and language techniques in a text.

☐ I can analyse the features of a narrative climax.

☐ I can create an atmosphere of terror in my creative writing.

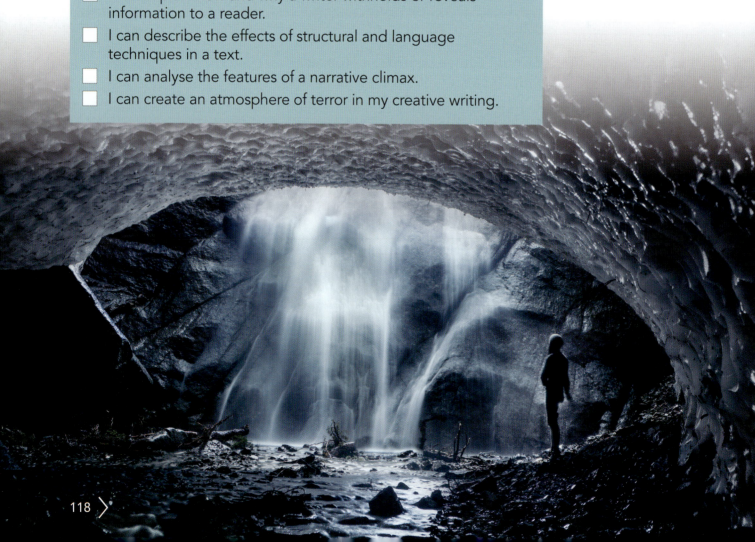

Check your progress

Answer these questions.

1   When planning an informative article for specific audiences, what should you consider before you write?

2   Give three different techniques you could use in a persuasive speech.

3   What aspects of language help to create the voice of a text?

4   Give a definition of dystopian fiction.

5   What advice would you give to another learner about when and where to use complex words in a written text?

6   'Writers decide the level of knowledge they allow a reader to have'. Explain what this means.

Project

What do you think the people in the year 3000 will think about the world you live in? What would you like them to know about life now? Art, music, books, films, photographs and other items reflect the cultures that people live in. They are all ways of recording people's values and interests. Which items would you choose to represent your culture?

In groups of four, you are going to give a presentation. You will describe eight items that represent aspects of your culture.

Start by researching various items in your group. Make a long list and then narrow it down to eight items that you think give the best and most comprehensive representation of your culture. Collect these items, or find images of them.

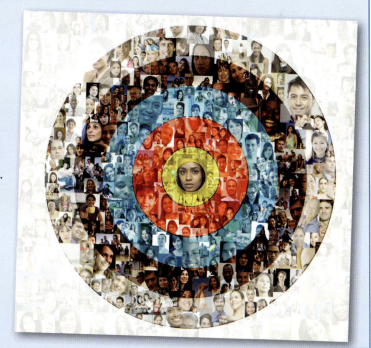

Give a presentation to the class. Each member of the group should introduce and describe two items. You must explain why these items are important. Use media and visual aids to support your presentation if you have access to them.

5 ▷ Heroes

In this unit, you will consider what makes a hero in both fiction and real life. You will discuss the qualities of heroes, read accounts of people who act heroically and write a film script about a superhero.

〉 5.1 Defining heroes

In this session, you will:

- identify explicit and implicit information in a text
- discuss and interpret different views of heroism
- explore the language and structure of argument texts
- write an effective argument.

Getting started

What do we mean when we call someone a 'hero'? What qualities do heroes have? What recent news stories can you think of that have featured people doing heroic things? Discuss your ideas in small groups.

What is a hero?

Most people have similar ideas about what a hero is, but they may disagree about which people are worthy of being called heroes. Read this magazine article – a non-fiction text that discusses heroism. Remember that discussion texts present information and explore a topic from different **perspectives**.

Modern heroes

Why does a modern society need heroes? Arundhati Adiga explores our need for heroes.

'Hero' was originally an ancient Greek word. It meant 'defender' – a person who protects and saves people and places from attack. The way we use the word 'hero' in our modern world shares some of that sense: a woman who saves people from a burning building is a hero and a man who jumps in front of a bullet to save another person is a hero. But what about sportspeople, musicians and celebrities? Are they heroes?

A poem written nearly 3000 years ago by the Greek poet Homer tells the story of the soldier Odysseus who spends ten years trying to return to his family after a long war abroad. Along the way, he faces many tests and difficulties. He battles monsters, is punished, tempted and controlled by gods and strange creatures, but he takes on whatever challenges lie in his path. Societies choose their heroes to reflect their values – the ancient Greeks valued bravery and determination. Homer gave his hero these qualities so the Greeks would admire this character and be interested in his adventures.

But who are today's heroes? We don't seem to face the same difficulties as Odysseus – or do we? Perhaps the 'monsters' we face today are things like war and poverty. Many modern societies regard soldiers as heroes because they are willing to die in defence of their country. Some people value those who stand up for important issues. Martin Luther King (1929–68) and Sojourner Truth (1797–1883) fought for equal rights for black people and women, as both of these groups suffered severe **discrimination**.

> **Key word**
>
> **perspective:** the 'angle' that a story or account is told from – whose 'eyes' the reader sees it through

> **discrimination:** when people are treated unfairly, often because of their race, sex or age

Others see medical researchers or environmental campaigners as heroes, working to rescue people from disease or to save the planet.

Research suggests that heroes have six key qualities: **leadership**, loyalty, determination, bravery, selflessness and a willingness to take big risks when needed. When people admire a hero, they do so because he or she embodies an ideal set of characteristics that they would like to have themselves. So next time you decide to **hero-worship** somebody, think about what your choice says about you.

leadership: being a good leader

hero-worship: strongly admire

Speaking tip

Remember that in a group discussion, it is important – and interesting – to explore points that you disagree on. Take turns to speak, and be respectful of other people's opinions. Try to find out *why* someone thinks differently from you. This will help you understand the issues you are discussing more fully.

1   Reread the article. Choose an appropriate way to make notes to answer the following questions.

   a   Why is Odysseus the ideal hero for ancient Greeks?

   b   What types of people do others regard as heroes in modern times?

   c   What are the six qualities of a hero?

   d   What does the writer mean when he says, the hero *embodies an ideal set of characteristics that they would like to have themselves*?

2   In groups of four, discuss your own views on modern heroes.

   •   Suggest some people who might be called a hero.

   •   Discuss whether or not they show the six qualities mentioned in the article.

   •   Debate whether the six qualities are a useful way of defining heroes. What other important qualities should a hero have?

False heroes

Argument writing outlines a series of reasons to persuade readers to agree with a point of view. Argument writing and persuasive writing share many features, but argument writing often has a more forceful tone.

Read this article, which argues that celebrities are not true heroes.

The age of false heroes

Do we **worship** false heroes? Of course we do. Ask a young person to name a hero and they won't name an explorer or one of the great medical scientists. No, they'll name a celebrity – somebody whose only real claim to fame is that they are famous.

Celebrities may appear to have things in common with true heroes. For example, they are often highly **motivated**. However, even though their sporting or musical achievements may be impressive, the motivation that celebrities have is entirely selfish. They do it because they want to be worshipped or rich, or most likely both. Real heroes are unselfish.

Although some celebrities contribute to charity, think about the real reason behind such donations. It's for publicity. Celebrities need fame and **air time**: it's essential for their career, so big acts of charity are usually timed to happen at the same time as their music or film releases. Hardly **heroic**, is it?

So what do celebrities contribute? Not much. Although actors say lines in front of a camera and musicians perform songs, none of these things helps society. At best, celebrities entertain us; but some celebrities are immoral. Check out rap lyrics: boastful, offensive and aggressive. They're as far from heroism as you can get.

In the end, celebrity is always about money. The heroes we must admire are those not driven by fame and fortune. Our heroes must be unselfish, brave and willing to give up their lives for others.

> **worship:** to show great admiration towards someone or something
>
> **motivated:** enthusiastic
>
> **air time:** appearances on media
>
> **heroic:** having the qualities of a hero

3   List the main points of the argument.

Language focus

Conjunctions are useful words that help to structure sentences. **Coordinating conjunctions** ('and, 'but', 'or') are used in compound sentences. In argument texts, they can be used to join parts of an argument and help build it up – for example:

- Real heroes are always thinking about other people <u>and</u> they never do things for fame.

Some **subordinating conjunctions** (for example, 'although', 'while', 'despite') are used to introduce a contradiction. In argument texts, they may be used for effect to set up a particular point of view and then suggest that view is wrong. Subordinating conjunctions can be used in different positions in a sentence:

- People often think celebrities are good people, <u>although</u> there are many times when celebrities misbehave.

- <u>Although</u> celebrities can distract us for an hour, they contribute nothing to society.

Key words

coordinating conjunction: a word such as 'and', 'but', 'or' that joins two words or two main clauses in a sentence

subordinating conjunction: a word such as 'although' or 'while' that joins a main clause to a subordinate clause in a sentence

---

4   Effective argument writing relies on a strong voice as well as a convincing viewpoint. In this article, the writer's personality and opinion come across clearly.

Find the following language features in the article. Write down the effect that each one has on the argument being presented and on the reader.

- emotive words

- positive and negative vocabulary

- questions and answers

- triples

- coordinating and subordinating conjunctions

- imperatives

- **modal verbs**.

5   Write a **counter-argument** to the one in 'The age of false heroes', in which you argue that sportspeople, actors and musicians *do* have heroic qualities. Write 150 words, using standard English.

Key words

modal verb: one of nine verbs used to show possibility – 'can', 'may', 'must', 'shall', 'will', 'could', 'might', 'should', 'would'

counter-argument: an argument that presents an opposing viewpoint

- First, plan your argument – make a list of points you want to include.

- Then think about the best order to present these points in your writing.

- Finally, draft your argument, using conjunctions to link and build your points, and any other techniques you have learnt.

Self-assessment

Read your argument carefully.

- Have you created a clear, forceful voice?
- How many of the techniques for creating an effective argument have you used?
- Which additional ones could you include to improve your writing?

Redraft your writing to improve it.

Summary checklist

☐ I can identify and explain explicit and implicit meanings in a text.

☐ I can comment on and interpret different views of heroism.

☐ I can identify features of argument writing and comment on their effect.

☐ I can write an effective argument, using appropriate language and structural features.

> 5.2 Looking for Charlie

In this session, you will:

- consider how writers combine techniques for overall effect
- combine techniques in your own writing to create specific effects
- discuss how ideas of heroism are reflected in a character
- write a personal response to a character.

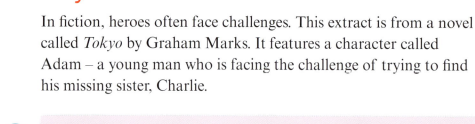

Getting started

Look at this picture. In pairs, discuss why the person might be termed a 'hero'. What personal qualities does he seem to have?

Tokyo

In fiction, heroes often face challenges. This extract is from a novel called *Tokyo* by Graham Marks. It features a character called Adam – a young man who is facing the challenge of trying to find his missing sister, Charlie.

Extract 1

Adam stood in the street, looking at the night-time version of **Asakusa** going on around him. Then he gazed up at the sky, expecting stars, but in a different pattern to the one he'd see at home.

Nothing, just black. No stars. **Neon** all the way.

A whole world of neon. Every colour of the rainbow, except the subtle ones. Flashing on and off, rising and falling like electronic, coloured rain … pictures, symbols, graphics, all glowing in the night. And the occasional English words, just to add to the confusion.

Was everyone here talking to someone else on a mobile phone? It certainly looked that way, with those not talking deeply involved in texting. Adam wondered what a Japanese text message looked like. Very different. Like now. Nothing looked the same as it had during the day and Adam suddenly felt completely **disorientated**.

What had he done, coming here? How was he ever going to have a chance of finding Charlie in this madhouse – what had he been thinking? As the world flowed around him, it occurred to Adam that he had two choices: go home, the first chance he had, or have a go at doing what he'd come here for.

> **Asakusa:** district of Tokyo
>
> **neon:** describing very bright colours, often in lights
>
> **disorientated:** confused about which direction to go in

If he didn't actually make a move, *do* something, he felt like he'd still be standing on this bit of pavement, **dithering**, when the sun came up. He'd already figured out that the tube map in the guidebook was much harder to make sense of than the one included in the fold-out city map he'd bought; standing in a pool of streetlight he took another look, seeing that he was actually just eleven stops from **Roppongi**. It could not be that difficult a journey to do, and he'd at least be able to start his search for the Bar Belle and feel he hadn't wasted the whole of his first day in Tokyo.

> **dithering:** not making a decision; wasting time
>
> **Roppongi:** district of Tokyo

1   The beginning of this extract focuses on the setting. It has been written in a way that shows Adam's confusion at finding himself in this place. Reread the first five paragraphs and answer these questions.

   a   Why does the writer use minor sentences in paragraph 2?

   b   How do you interpret the use of figurative language (*madhouse*) in paragraph 5?

2   Writers often combine features to create effects. This means that techniques such as figurative language, punctuation choices and sentence types work together to create an overall impact.

Write an analysis of the techniques used in paragraph 3, including simile, ellipsis, lists, and the use of commas and sentence types. Explain the overall effect that the combination of these features creates.

3   Write your own paragraph about a character in a challenging setting. Combine a variety of techniques to create a similar effect to the one in the opening of *Tokyo*.

- When you are given freedom to choose your own character and setting, how easy do you find it?
- What process did you go through to decide what your character and setting should be?

Now read the next part of the story.

Extract 2

Underground there was a new world, a bright, clean environment which, considering the neon mayhem going on above it, was astonishingly free of **excessive** advertising. Working out how to buy a ticket, though, had proved to be no easy job – even after he'd found the button which changed the Japanese characters on the text screen into English. Luckily someone who turned out to understand more English than they actually spoke spotted him standing, confused, in front of a bank of ticket machines, and between them they'd managed to buy a ticket that Adam hoped would get him to Roppongi and back again.

After the frustrating ticket-buying experience, the journey turned out to be **a breeze**, just a question of paying attention and following instructions and numbers, of going from A18 to E23, through colour-coded tunnels and on south-bound trains. Simple.

Exiting Roppongi station Adam found himself back in Neon City and at what appeared to be a major crossroads. And somewhere here there was a place called the Bar Belle, where Alice and Charlie had been working, and where Alice had last seen Charlie walking out with a customer.

The only problem was he had absolutely no idea where in Roppongi – no small area – to find the Bar Belle. Before leaving England he'd looked it up on the Net, but found nothing. Was it too small? He'd have to find it first to know, but how? Then, above the roar of the traffic, he heard a badly amplified voice calling out, something about music. Now he looked he could see that there were quite a few people, one of them might know something. Whether they'd tell him was another matter entirely.

> **excessive:** an unnecessary amount of something
>
> **a breeze:** very easy

4   In the 'Getting started' activity, you discussed a picture of a firefighter and the concept of heroism. How does Adam compare to this idea of heroism in the extracts you have read so far? What, if any, heroic qualities does Adam display?

In pairs, discuss Adam's actions and the way he responds to his situation.

5   Some readers would not regard Adam as a 'hero'. Here is one learner's opinion of him:

Adam really struggles to cope with his challenges – he's not really much of a hero.

How do you react to this opinion? Write a paragraph explaining whether you agree or disagree with it. Use quotations from the extracts to support your view.

Summary checklist

- [ ] I can identify and analyse different techniques used to create an overall effect.
- [ ] I can use literary and linguistic techniques to create an effective setting.
- [ ] I can develop a discussion by listening to and sharing ideas on a topic.
- [ ] I can express an opinion about a character, using relevant quotations to support my ideas.

Writing tip

When using quotations, embed them in your writing. This means choosing short, relevant quotations and including them in your sentences in a way that is grammatically correct.

> 5.3 Danger?

In this session, you will:

- explore how writers create realistic dialogue
- consider how language can be used to present character
- comment on the effects of a structural pattern in a story
- write an imaginative blog.

Getting started

When people speak to each other in real life, it is rarely fluent. In pairs, have a conversation about a city you have both visited or would like to visit. As you talk, focus on *how* you are speaking. Did either of you use **fillers**, **discourse markers** or non-standard English?

In the next part of *Tokyo*, Adam encounters another man. This character establishes both the multicultural nature of the setting and a sense of mystery in the plot.

Key words

filler: a non-word, such as 'er' or 'um', or a phrase such as 'you know', used to fill pauses in speech

discourse marker: a word used to separate speech into sections, such as 'right' or 'so'

Extract 3

Adam chose the least threatening-looking of the guys and hoped you could **judge this particular book by its cover**. He approached, friendly, smiling. 'Speak English, man?'

'Chor, wa'choo wan?' All teeth and big smiles, the man thrust a coloured flyer at Adam.

'I need to find the Bar Belle, I'm meeting a friend there and I lost the address.'

'Piece a dirt place, man.'

Adam dug into his jeans pocket and brought out one of the ¥1,000 notes he'd stuffed in there after buying his subway ticket. 'I really don't care …'

The man reached out to take it and Adam moved his hand back. 'OK, right … OK, man, see, you go cross da street, you take secon right, you fine it up a few floors, five or six, I don 'member zackly. Look for da sign, man.'

'Thanks.' Adam handed over the note.

> **judge this particular book by its cover:** work out the man's personality from his appearance

1   The writer uses **phonetic spelling** to show the way the man pronounces words and phrases. For example, 'Chor, wa'choo wan?' would be written in standard English as 'Sure, what do you want?'.

In pairs, translate the man's dialogue into standard English. To help you, start by saying the words out loud.

> **Key words**
>
> **phonetic spelling:** spelling words as they sound

2   Writers use dialogue to reveal the personality of characters and to show how they interact. In Extract 3, Adam and the man he meets talk differently. Although Adam's dialogue includes some informal features, such as contractions (*I'm*), his speech is closer to standard English.

Write a paragraph explaining:

- the techniques the writer uses to show these two different voices, including standard and non-standard English; ellipsis; **elision**

- The effect on the story of including characters with different types of dialogue – what do these choices add?

> **Key word**
>
> **elision:** missing out letters from words

Reading tip

Remember that word choice can have an effect on the wider text. For example, it can help to suggest things about character, add realism, create atmosphere, show differences and conflicts and add detail to the story setting.

Now read the next part of the story. Adam is in an alley. He has not been able to find Bar Belle.

Extract 4

Adam turned to go back up the way he'd come, and stopped. **Silhouetted** against the bright lights he saw a figure that seemed to be looking his way, waiting … Had he been set up here? More than likely. He looked behind him, back into the gloom of what looked like a dead end; no point in running down there, then. He cast around in the shadow on the ground for anything he might be able to use to defend himself, and saw nothing.

Walking slowly back up the alley Adam thought about trying to fit some coins between his fingers like he'd seen done in a movie, but he knew he was clutching at straws now. Best just go for this head on, wait until the last minute and make a rush for the street and hope he got past the guy. He'd be safe out in the crowds. Safer, anyway.

He'd been **psyching himself** up so much that it was only when he was just about to start running, possibly yelling at the top of his voice, that he realised the person was not only standing with his back to the alley, not looking down it at all, he was also much nearer to the street than he'd realised. And, as the man turned to look to his right, Adam could now see he was quite an old guy.

The feeling of panic **subsided**, replaced by one of embarrassment as he walked past the man and out on to the pavement; how stupid would he have felt, tearing past this total stranger like a madman? Total **dimwit** stupid.

Accompanied by an odd sense of anticlimax, Adam made his way back to the big junction and the subway station.

silhouetted: shown as a dark shape

psyching himself: mentally preparing himself

subsided: faded away

dimwit: a foolish person; someone who is not clever

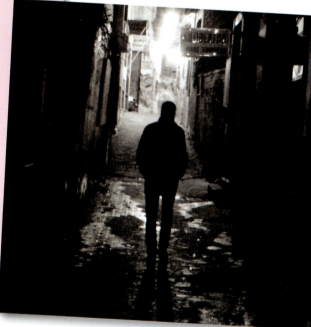

3   In this extract, the writer introduces another man. His presence creates tension and helps the reader understand how Adam feels about the world in which he has found himself. In pairs, discuss these questions:

   a   In the first paragraph, the writer focuses on visual descriptions of the man and the alley. Using examples, explain the effect of this.

   b   In the second paragraph, Adam prepares to fight but says he was *clutching at straws*. What does this mean?

   c   Describe Adam's different feelings in paragraphs 3 and 4.

   d   In the final paragraph, Adam feels an *odd sense of anticlimax*.

   Explain what this means and what it tells you about Adam's character.

4   The writer structures this extract by first creating tension, then building it, then releasing that tension. In pairs:

   •   identify lines where the tension is built up

   •   identify lines where the tension is released.

   What effect does this 'tension-and-release' structure have on the reader?

What do you find challenging about identifying the effects of a structural pattern?

5   Fictional heroes usually find themselves under pressure and facing challenges. To make their heroes realistic, writers may present them with weaknesses and uncertainties. In *Tokyo*, we see Adam experiencing a range of emotions.

   Imagine you are Adam. Write a 200-word blog explaining what has happened to you so far and how your search has made you feel. Use the opening lines here, then continue your blog in the same style. Focus on using words, punctuation and sentences for effect.

For example, you could use non-standard English to recreate the dialogue, or manipulate the structure of your account to create the feeling of tension-and-release. You could start like this:

> **No luck yet**
>
> I arrived in Tokyo with a mission – to find Charlie. So far, she's still missing, but I have discovered a lot about myself. Being in Tokyo at night was weird.

Once you have drafted your writing, edit and redraft as necessary to improve it.

Summary checklist

- [ ] I can identify features that make dialogue realistic.
- [ ] I can analyse how language is used to present a character in a piece of fiction.
- [ ] I can write about the effects of a structural pattern in a story.
- [ ] I can write an imaginative blog.

> 5.4 Young heroes

In this session, you will:

- listen and respond to information about a young carer
- compare two accounts on a similar theme, noting similarities and differences
- explore the purpose, language and structural features of advice texts
- write an advice text using appropriate features.

Getting started

Many fiction and non-fiction news stories feature young people acting heroically. In pairs, make a list of examples and the qualities that young heroes have.

1 Young carers perform heroic acts every day. They face difficult circumstances and do everything they can to help the people they love who are facing problems.

Listen to Martika's story and make notes on what this young carer does and how she feels about her situation.

Life as a young carer

Now read a newspaper article by Kate Hilpern that describes the experiences of another young carer. Her experience is a bit different from Martika's.

 # A Young Carer's Story

Sarah Thomas, 18, started looking after her mother, who has MS, from a very early age, and later became her dad's carer too. But she isn't bitter about missing out on the parts of growing up that others take for granted.

'I've never known anything else,' says Sarah, who is now 18 and who continues to do everything from general household chores to helping with medication, providing physical assistance, filling in forms and many other day-to-day jobs. 'It's hard to say what I'd have been like if I hadn't cared for her from a young age, I do know I'm very independent – far more so than most of my friends.'

It's true that Sarah's confidence, **assertiveness**, **empathy** and **buoyancy** all combine to make her seem much older than her teenage years, while her relationship with both parents reveals a rare mixture of easiness and **frankness**.

There are lots of assumptions made about young carers, says Sarah, not least that they miss out on holidays. 'In fact, we usually got away three times a year. Then there's the assumption that my education suffered. But I did well in my GCSEs and am enjoying studying health and social care at college. If anything, I hand in work early.'

The worst aspect of Sarah's life has been bullying by her peers. 'I've never yet met a young carer who hasn't been bullied. I think it's because we stand out – we have often had to grow up quicker than our peers, and kids don't always like that. In my case, there was a group who targeted me physically and verbally at school.'

Listening tip

When listening to personal accounts, organise your notes by separating your page into two columns – facts and feelings.

MS: multiple sclerosis, a disease that damages nerve cells

assertiveness: confident (sometimes forceful) behaviour

empathy: the ability to understand other people's feelings

buoyancy: optimistic attitude

frankness: being honest and direct

Sarah first started meeting other young carers when she helped to set up a local group for them, when she was eight. 'It became my lifeline. Best of all, it was where we got to be children. Play was a major part of those **get-togethers**.'

get-togethers: meetings

2   Make a list of the negative and positive aspects of Sarah's life as a young carer.

3   Write a paragraph explaining the similarities and differences between Martika's and Sarah's experiences of caring. Use examples from the notes you made in Activity 1 to show these differences.

Supporting young carers

Now read another online article by Liz Burton. This one has a different purpose – to give British teachers advice on how they can help and support young carers in their school.

As a teacher, you are well positioned to help students who are young carers. You can provide more support in their studies, help them access social support, or simply **lend an ear**.

lend an ear: listen to someone

jealousy: being unhappy or mean because someone has something that you do not

Here are ways you can support young carers in your school.

1. Invite students to talk

Pay particular attention to quiet students, whose silence may result from their exhaustion or worry. However, it's important to share your interest with the rest of the class too. This prevents **jealousy** and avoids drawing attention to a struggling student.

2. Support their studies

Young carers will likely need support in school to keep up with their peers and get the most out of their education. You should make an effort to provide them with extra help whenever they need it.

To support their studies, you could:

- Run a lunchtime catch-up class. Use this time to go through homework or any topics the student didn't quite understand.

- Allow students to use their phone during breaks and lunch to check on the person they're caring for.

- Be sympathetic with problems, such as lateness and missed homework.

3. Help them access support

Most young carers won't know that there are numerous support **avenues** available for them.

The types of support young carers can access include:

Mental and physical health support. Help the student arrange an appointment with the school nurse and/or **counsellor** to discuss their issues and ways to cope with their situation.

Socialising with other young carers. Meeting other young carers can be an excellent way for the student to make new friends. The Children's Society runs such social clubs and support services for young carers in many areas.

Do your best to help those students in need if you ever notice signs or they open up to you. You'll help the young carer, and the person they care for, live more **fulfilling** lives.

---

avenues: options
counsellor: someone who offers support and advice for people who need them
fulfilling: satisfying or happy

Language focus

People read advice texts because they want guidance on how to do something. It is important that the advice is written simply and clearly, so writers often use imperative sentences, which give clear instructions on what to do. For example:

- <u>Give</u> young carers extra time to do their homework.

The imperative verb 'give' leaves no room for doubt about what the reader should do.

Continued

However, in advice texts, readers may also need guidance on different possible situations, and to understand whether something is essential or just preferable. Modal verbs – 'can', 'may', 'must', 'shall', 'will', 'could', 'might', 'should', 'would' – are useful for this. For example:

- You <u>must</u> help a young carer cope with school.

'Must' makes it clear that the advice has to be followed.

- Teachers <u>should</u> be aware that young carers <u>may</u> get tired easily.

'Should' is less forceful, as if the writer is simply reminding the reader. 'May' shows that it is a possibility (not a certainty) that young carers tire easily.

4   In this article, the writer uses a range of organisational features to sequence the information. In pairs, discuss and make notes on the structure and language of the article. Look for the following features and discuss the combined effect they have:

- headings, subheadings, numbers and bullet points

- imperative verbs and modal verbs.

5   Using the information from the texts in this session, write an advice text aimed at young carers. The purpose is to advise them how they can cope with their situation. Make sure readers know that help is available. Use details from Activity 1 and 'Life as a young carer' to show that there are some positive aspects to being a young carer. Remember that advice texts use:

- clear, straightforward language

- imperative verbs and modal verbs

- a range of structural devices such as subheadings, bullets and numbered lists.

Choose language and a level of formality that suits your purpose and audience. Write 200 words.

Self-assessment

Read your draft. Have you:

- given advice using words your audience will understand?
- used imperative and modal verbs accurately?
- used a range of structural features?

Summary checklist

☐ I can make notes on information from an aural account.

☐ I can identify similarities and differences in two accounts on the same topic.

☐ I can identify and comment on the features of advice texts.

☐ I can write an advice text using appropriate language and structural features.

> 5.5 Superheroes

In this session, you will:

- explore the features of superhero stories
- consider aspects of voice
- compare and summarise genre conventions based on different accounts
- devise your own superhero storyline.

Getting started

What qualities do you associate with superheroes?
What are typical settings for superhero stories?
Discuss your ideas in pairs. The images on the
next page may help you.

Continued

Superhero movies

Superhero films feature very different heroes from the ones you have studied so far. In this type of film, aspects of character and plot are often **exaggerated** for effect. Typically, the main character and the situations they find themselves in are highly unusual. Read this article, which describes superhero films.

A super-real type of film

Superhero films go *way*, *way* beyond realism. Way beyond. And while we know the stories are unbelievable, it's hard not to be entertained by them. Who doesn't feel excited when the superhero saves the world yet again? Who isn't fascinated by the character's backstory? Well … maybe not fascinated, but certainly entertained!

Superhero films might feel a bit predictable, but that's part of their appeal. They are stories about secret identities. They are stories of ordinary people who transform into extraordinary crime-fighters in colourful costumes. The contrast between the two versions of the same person is usually vast. That said, the 'disguise' they wear is pretty unconvincing (at least to the audience – the other characters never see through it!).

You've probably noticed that there's always some reason for the character's superpower. It might be the result of an accident, as with Spider-Man, or it could be the death of parents that causes the

superhero to develop their superpower, as with Batman. When they get their powers, these guys soon discover that it's not easy being a superhero. Superhero films usually include a scene where the character struggles with their secret identity, often while hiding in their secret **lair**.

Once they accept their new powers, the main story focuses on a conflict between the superhero and a supervillain – a super-nasty person – usually over control of the world. And of course, the superhero wins. Nothing distracts him – except, of course, the pretty girl who admires him but somehow doesn't know his secret …

lair: a hideout

1   Summarise the conventions of the superhero genre. Use what you know about recognising main and subsidiary points to identify the main points the writer makes about the content of the films.

Peer assessment

Swap ideas with a partner and compare your summaries.

- How many conventions have they identified?
- Have you identified the same features or different ones?

2   This article is written in a light-hearted voice – as if the writer is drawing attention to the unrealistic content of superhero films.

Working in pairs:

a   Find examples of phrases and uses of punctuation that are playful.

b   Discuss whether you think the writer is criticising the genre or not.

Stan Lee's superheroes

These two extracts are from different articles. They describe the superheroes devised by Stan Lee, a famous comic-book creator.

Stan Lee's final creation was a Chinese superhero

Comic book legend Stan Lee is known as the force behind Spider-Man, the Hulk and the X-Men, but his final creation was a Chinese female superhero.

Named 'Jewel', the character is a world-touring pop star by day and a superhero in disguise by night. But it is unclear whether Lee had decided on her superpowers before he passed away.

The first major Chinese character in Lee's comics appeared in the 1960s comic Tales of Suspense. Supervillain 'The Mandarin', born to a Chinese father and an English mother, once tried to destroy China's entire rice crop. He was stopped by Iron Man.

When Stan Lee created an Indian superhero to keep Mumbai safe

He was known for creating comic book icons such as the X-Men and Thor, but the legendary Stan Lee also co-created an Indian superhero.

In 2011, *Chakra: The Invincible* made his debut in a comic book.

The story had a touch of Spider-Man and Iron Man with a *desi* twist, as Chakra was a teenage tech genius named Raju Rai who **inadvertently** activated a blue jumpsuit that unleashed the chakras (energy centres) in his body. This suit gave him special powers to keep Mumbai safe.

> *desi:* Indian, Pakistani or Bangladeshi
> **inadvertently:** accidentally

3   Summarise the features of the superheroes found in these accounts. Do these characters follow the conventions you identified in Activity 1? If so, in what ways? How are they different?

4   Choose one of Stan Lee's two superheroes – 'Jewel' or 'Chakra'. Using your knowledge of the genre, work in pairs to suggest some storylines for them. Start by choosing a method to generate and organise your ideas about:

   • the hero's different superpowers

   • the supervillain they face

   • the settings in which the story could take place.

Enviros

Before scriptwriters begin writing, they provide an outline of the characters and plot so that film companies and producers know what the stories will be about. Read the outline of the beginning of a superhero film.

Enviros: the planet needs her!

Chun-hei is a bored schoolgirl who feels trapped in a world that doesn't care. The planet is dying, but everybody in the small town where she lives seems more concerned with making money. As a baby, Chun-hei was given a special gemstone from a mysterious, unknown person. Touching the gemstone allowed her to understand nature and the planet in a way every other human can't. When natural disasters seem likely to happen, she prevents them by changing into Enviros and averting danger. Her main skill is predicting disaster, but she also has extraordinary speed and strength. She can fly too. Her biggest challenge yet is the dangerous corporation boss Ron Punch, otherwise known as supervillain Arco. He has a plan to sell the world's resources to a nearby planet before destroying Earth.

5   Using this example as a model, write an outline of your ideas for a story about 'Jewel' or 'Chakra' based on Activity 4.

Summary checklist

- [ ] I can identify the conventions of the superhero genre.
- [ ] I can comment on aspects of voice.
- [ ] I can summarise and compare information from different accounts on the same topic.
- [ ] I can plan and write a plot and character outline for a superhero film.

> 5.6 Scripting stories

In this session, you will:

- read a film script in groups
- explore the structural and language features of film scripts
- plan and write a scene from a film.

Getting started

In groups, act out a favourite scene from a film. Think about the way you speak and perform. Afterwards, discuss what makes the scene so enjoyable.

Reading tip

When reading an unseen text aloud, use punctuation cues to help you express the meaning correctly. For example, emphasise the pauses indicated by commas and full stops. These pauses are also good points to vary the tone of your voice, which helps speech sound more expressive.

1 Film scripts are different from scripts written for the stage. Stage plays are performed in small spaces and they rely heavily on the dialogue and movement of actors to communicate what is happening. Film is a very visual format – the story can be told or implied by images that the camera shows. Film scripts therefore contain a lot of information about scenery and action.

In groups of four, read aloud the film script for a scene from *Enviros*. Three people should take the role of the characters and one person should read the detailed descriptions of setting. Concentrate on reading accurately and with expression.

Enviros

An establishing shot of the outside of a large school. Inside, a bell rings and boys and girls are leaving class. Close-up shot of Chun-hei sitting behind a desk looking tired. Her teacher, Mr Yeung pulls up a chair.

MR YEUNG: Are you going to tell me what's going on? You're my best student, but you've been distracted. Your grades are slipping, Chun-hei.

Chun-hei looks out of the window. We see things from her point of view here – the top of part of the sky is turning purple and

establishing shot: the first image in a sequence, which shows the viewer where the scene is taking place

close-up shot: an image focusing closely on a small part of a scene

a strong wind begins. Chun-hei looks anxious. She needs to be outside.

CHUN-HEI: It's nothing, sir. Can I go?

MR YEUNG: Of course. Let me know if I can help. See you tomorrow.

As he says this, Chun-hei is already on the move. We now see an outside view of the school. Chun-hei is running in the opposite direction to other students, towards the sports hall, bumping into some of them.

Interior shot of the empty sports hall. We see a close-up of Chun-hei's eyes, which are widening. She is transforming into Enviros. Next, we see an exterior shot of the school from above. Suddenly, Enviros flies past.

The scene changes to the interior of Ron Punch's large office. It has a long, floor-to-ceiling window. There are skyscrapers outside. Punch is at his desk, a large snake crawling across it. He is talking angrily over the office telephone.

PUNCH: Well, make it happen ... I don't want to hear that. I don't pay you to tell me you can't do things. Do it and do it now.

Punch slams the phone down and walks to the window. He speaks aloud to himself.

PUNCH: If this goes to plan, I'll be off this stinking planet in plenty of time to watch it burn.

Enviros lands on the roof of Punch's skyscraper. We see her green costume and watch her walk confidently to the side of the building. Although it is 60 storeys high, she begins to slide down the front of the building. We next see her from Punch's point of view as she appears on the outside of the window, staring directly at him. They are separated by a sheet of glass.

PUNCH: You! Prepare to die.

> **interior shot:** an image showing the inside of a building
>
> **exterior shot:** an image showing the outside of a building

2   What structural features are there in the film script? In pairs, discuss and make notes on how the writer has organised the script. Consider:

- the order in which the events take place
- the type and range of settings
- the balance between speech and description
- the amount of dialogue each character has.

3   Now look closely at the language choices in the script. In pairs, find examples of the following features. Discuss why they are used and what effect they have:

- vocabulary relating to films and film-making
- the verb tense in the descriptions
- the use of prepositions and nouns in the descriptions
- the use of imperatives
- the contrasting voices of Chun-hei and Punch.

4   Using your notes, write a summary of the language and structural features of a film script.

Explain the impact of some of these features. How do they help the reader understand characters and action?

5   Think back to the outline you created for a film about Chakra or Jewel in Session 5.5. You are now going to write a script based on your plot ideas.

Start by choosing a key moment in a superhero film that you will create as a script, such as the point when the character's backstory is revealed, or a dramatic battle with a supervillain.

- First, plan the story. You could draw a **storyboard** or write a bullet-point list of the main events.
- Then draft your script. Remember to use the features you identified earlier in this session and to spend time making sure the descriptions are clear and detailed.

Write 150 words.

> **Key word**
>
> **storyboard:**
> (in films and television) a series of drawings or images showing the planned order of events in a story

Writing tip

When planning any narrative, sketching a quick storyboard is a useful way to map out your ideas. Each box in your storyboard should show a key moment in the plot – one of the big 'blocks' of the story. You do not have to spend a lot of time on this, just use it as a quick way of visualising your ideas.

6   Read your draft script with a partner. If possible, record the reading and listen to it afterwards to help you make decisions about redrafting. After reading each other's scripts, discuss:

- if it is clear what is happening in the story

- whether the features of a film script have been used

- how the script could be improved.

Redraft your script before handing in a final version.

Summary checklist

☐ I can contribute effectively to a group performance of a film script.

☐ I can identify and comment on the effect of the structural and language features of film scripts.

☐ I can plan, write and evaluate an effective film script.

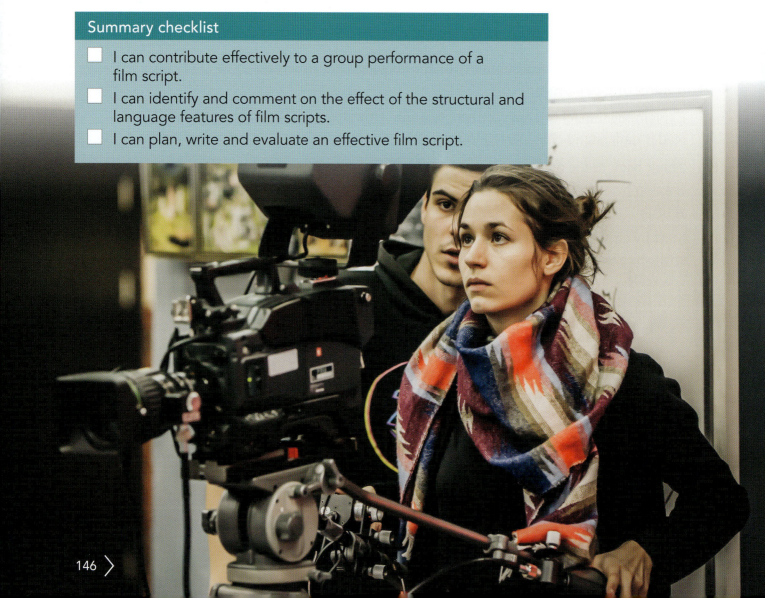

Check your progress

Answer these questions.

1 'Heroes have six key qualities: leadership, loyalty, determination, bravery, selflessness, and a willingness to take massive risks when needed'. In your own words, explain what these six words mean.

2 Using an example, explain how combining different techniques can create effects such as tension.

3 Explain the effects created by using non-standard English in dialogue.

4 Describe some of the ways that advice texts are written and structured.

5 What are the conventions of superhero stories?

6 What advice would you give to explain how to set out a film script?

Project

Who would you include in a list of modern real-life heroes? In this project, you are going to work in a group and give a talk about a hero.

An international company wants to make a series of short films about modern heroes. The film series will be called *My 21st Century Hero*. They want young people to talk about somebody they admire – a figure from a sporting, musical, creative, scientific or environmental background. They must have been alive in the 21st century.

As a group, your task is to persuade the international company to make a film about your chosen hero. Start by discussing and researching possible heroes that you could talk about, after which you must agree on *one* hero to present. Once you have done this, prepare your talk.

Each person in the group must say something about the hero, including their background, what they have achieved and why they are admired. Most importantly, you need to persuade the company why they should make a film about your hero.

The talk should last five minutes.

6 ▸ Monsters

In this unit, you will read accounts of different monsters and explore things that people are afraid of. You will read fiction about a giant, poetry about a fearsome creature and an article about a monster below the ground created by humans.

> 6.1 A modern monster

In this session, you will:

- identify the main points in an article about a monstrous animal
- consider a writer's attitude towards the topic they are explaining
- explore the effect of emotive language on readers
- write your own account of a modern myth.

Getting started

In pairs, write a list of monsters and scary creatures you know of from books and films. What qualities do these creatures share? Do you enjoy reading this type of story? Why or why not? Discuss your ideas.

The hunt for Chupacabra

Accounts of mysterious monsters can be found in every culture. This article explains the background to a creature called the Chupacabra from Puerto Rico.

Extract 1

The world's first 'internet monster' – a cruel creature that empties the blood from its animal victims – has been caught …

Humans are fascinated and frightened by monster stories. We love hearing about strange, shadowy creatures that bring fear to communities around the world. Most societies have legends like this. In Mongolia, the Death Worm is a huge red creature that spits acid at its victims. In Colombia, Alligator Man swims along the coast looking for human wives. In Japan, man-eating spiders disguise themselves as attractive women before **devouring** their victims. And then in Puerto Rico, there's the feared Chupacabra …

Chupacabra means 'goat sucker' in Spanish, because this monster buries its teeth into animals, but descriptions of the creature vary. Typically (as with most supposed monsters), no photographs or footprints of the original Chupacabra exist – there's just a handful of eyewitness reports and a lot of dead animals. When the creature was first reported in 1995, it was said to have glowing red eyes, huge claws, spikes along its back and the ability to leap large distances. Over the next five years, more Chupacabras were rumoured to have been seen in Spanish-speaking countries such as Argentina, Mexico and Chile. The description of the monster also changed: by 1998, it was a fierce, hairless dog.

Unusually, these later Chupacabra bodies were actually tested by real scientists, rather than the 'experts' on web forums. The creatures had been shot by farmers and, for once, modern science could examine not only the victims of a monster, but the monster itself. The reality was a little less exciting than the myth. A Chupacabra was pretty awful to look at – skinny, hairless and with burnt areas on its skin. However, tests proved beyond doubt that the Chupacabras that had been found were less exotic animals – dogs, coyotes and racoons. Skin infections had caused these animals to develop bald patches, and as they scratched, their skin became inflamed, giving them a **gruesome** appearance. In short, there was no Chupacabra. Of course, that was no real surprise to most people!

devouring: eating quickly

gruesome: causing horror

1   List the main pieces of information about the appearance and behaviour of Chupacabra in the different sightings.

2   In your own words, write down what the following phrases mean.

For each one, note down the effect the writer may have intended them to have.

   a   *Humans are fascinated and frightened by monster stories.*

   b   *The reality was a little less exciting than the myth.*

   c   *Of course, that was no real surprise to most people!*

3   In pairs, discuss the attitude the writer takes towards the subject. Make a list of words and phrases that reveal the writer's attitude.

> What approach did you take to identifying the words and phrases that reveal the writer's attitude?

Reading tip

When looking for the main points in a text, always keep the task focus in mind. Scan each paragraph to distinguish the main point from those that are less important. Underline or highlight the main points if possible. Alternatively, make notes of each point using a list or a table.

Now read the second part of the article.

Extract 2

The internet was crucial in the spread of the Chupacabra myth. Modern communication has allowed rumour and myth to spread rapidly. A decade earlier, before global communication was so easy, this monster would have remained a local legend. But stories on the internet are like wildfires – they burn out of control. People told and retold the stories, changing descriptions of the creature each time. Without photographic evidence, the accounts of the Chupacabra were impossible to confirm. They seemed so exaggerated that it was hard to believe they were true, as this eyewitness account from Chile shows:

'The thing that I remember most was its horrific red eyes. I only saw it for a second, but it looked at me and struck fear into my heart. Those eyes will stay with me forever. Every time I go to sleep, I see them. And the speed with which it moved was incredible. I've seen nothing like it before or since. Those sharp spikes on its back and its horrendous claws could do serious damage to someone. I'm only glad I was indoors when I saw it.'

In fact, details about the original sighting of Chupacabra in 1995 go some way to explaining how the myth took hold. The first person to report the creature was Madelyne Tolentino, from Canovanas in Puerto Rico. She reported seeing a frightening creature that looked like an alien from her window. Upon closer investigation, Tolentino's description was very like that of an alien creature featured in the film *Species*, which she had recently watched. It seems likely that she saw one of the real animals that had a skin disease, and her imagination got the better of her. Once her description had been repeated and exaggerated online, the Chupacabra myth was born.

4   The first paragraph uses the phrase *stories on the internet are like wildfires – they burn out of control*. In pairs, discuss how this simile could be interpreted and what effect it has.

Language focus

Emotive language means words and phrases intended to produce an emotional response in readers. Writers choose emotive words when they want readers to have a strong reaction to the text – for example, shock, anger or terror. For example:

- The creature used its claws to attack the sheep.

- The menacing creature slashed at the terrified sheep with its razor-sharp claws.

The first example describes the action in a straightforward way. The second is much more dramatic, using strong verb and adjective choices such as 'menacing', 'slash', 'terrified' and 'razor-sharp' to draw the reader into the scene and make them feel the horror and fear of the situation.

5   The eyewitness account of the Chupacabra is written in emotive language. Write a paragraph explaining the overall impact on the reader of the words and phrases the speaker uses.

6   Using both extracts from the article, write your own account of the Chupacabra myth. You should write 150 words. Focus on:

- the background to the original sighting

- how the internet played a part in the myth

- how science helped to clear up the myth.

> 6.2 Fear of monsters

In this session, you will:

- identify and summarise the main points in an informative text
- consider how purpose and audience influence the way a text is written
- produce a leaflet for a specific purpose and audience.

Getting started

How are advice leaflets presented? How are they set out? What grammatical features of advisory writing can you remember from Unit 5?

Fear of the dark

Read this online article by Joshua A. Krisch which explains why people are afraid of monsters. It includes the opinions of Peter Gray, a professor of psychology.

How Monsters Under the Bed Became a Common Childhood Fear

Your children are afraid of the dark, and they are certain that monsters live under their beds.

It's not because of horror films. It's because the dark *is* scary, and monsters *do* exist.

'It's no surprise that infants have some fear of the dark. Throughout our <u>evolutionary history</u>, the dark was dangerous.' Humans rely on vision above all other senses, Gray explains, and the dark placed us in danger for thousands of years. It follows that a healthy fear of the dark is deeply ingrained in the human **psyche**.

Humans are born with a handful of fears. From birth, we're afraid of falling from great heights and afraid of loud noises; shortly thereafter we acquire fear of snakes and spiders. Among our earliest learned fears is fear of the dark.

At nightfall, Gray says, we **instinctively** want to be tucked away in a cave or bedroom, surrounded by other people who might help us fend off an attack when our senses are at their worst. This is probably why small children cry when they're left alone in a dark room. 'Over the course of <u>natural selection</u>, infants who expressed fear of being left alone by crying out were more likely to survive,' he says.

Which accounts for fear of the dark, and explains why your child only becomes truly afraid of the dark once you leave the room. If a lion is going to attack, it'll be then.

> **psyche:** the mind
> **instinctively:** without conscious thought

1   Look at two terms that are underlined in the text. Research what they mean. In your own words, write a brief glossary.

2   You have been asked to give a very brief summary of why children are afraid of the dark. Identify the main points in the article and then summarise them using as few words as possible.

Peer assessment

Swap books with a partner. Read each other's work.

- Has your partner identified all the main points?
- Are there any subsidiary points that you do not think should have been included?
- Which of you has used the fewest words?

3 Articles can be found in many sources – in newspapers, magazines and online. They are written with different readers in mind and for different purposes.

- Who do you think is the intended audience for this article? Who would read it and why? Explain your answer using quotations.

- What type of article is this – what is its purpose? How is it meant to help the intended reader?

4 You have been asked by a health education company to design a leaflet giving parents advice about helping their child to overcome a fear of monsters. You have made the following notes from your initial research.

- Technical name for fear of monsters is 'teraphobia'.
- In the past, people were frightened of sea dragons.
- Listening to children's fears is essential.
- Fear of monsters normally disappears by age nine, although adults can still get scared at times.
- Watching horror films can make teenagers frightened.
- Children like rewards – reward them for 'bravery' with stickers and treats.
- Laughing at children's fears never helps.
- Asking a child to draw their monster can help them.
- Some children's monsters are inspired by cartoons or even neighbours.
- If a fear lasts for more than six months, it is officially a phobia.
- Having a bedtime routine helps children overcome fears – bath and stories help.

You can use information from the article, but you will need to rewrite it in a suitable way. Remember that some of the information may not be useful for your audience or purpose.

- Read through the notes in Activity 4 and the article – work out which bits will be most useful for your audience.

- Plan a structure for your leaflet – think about the order of your content.

5   Draft the text for your leaflet. Remember that your audience is parents who may be concerned about their children and are reading your leaflet because they want information, advice and reassurance. Consider the tone and level of formality you should use. Take care with spelling, using some of the strategies you learnt in Session 3.6 to spell words correctly.

Use the features of advisory texts that you learnt about in Session 5.4, including:

- headings, subheadings, bullet points and numbered lists

- clear, direct advice written in straightforward language

- imperative sentences and modal verbs.

> **Writing tip**
>
> It is important to structure a leaflet appropriately. Most advice leaflets start by giving general information before moving on to specific advice. Breaking information into separate sections using subheadings will help your reader.

Self-assessment

Read your draft and consider whether you have:
- provided clear advice to your readers
- structured your leaflet in an effective way.

---

6   Select some images that you could use in your leaflet. Use a search engine, books or your own imagination to decide on suitable pictures. Once you have completed your draft and selected images, edit your work before producing your final text. Try to make your leaflet look as attractive and convincing as possible.

Think about the various stages of producing your leaflet:
- Which parts did you enjoy most and why?
- Which other parts were most challenging and what did you learn from them?

> 6.3 The giant

In this session, you will:

- read a fable and identify the key features of the genre
- explore methods for presenting characters
- comment on figurative language, including symbols
- analyse how time connectives and sentence openings help structure a story.

Getting started

In pairs, discuss stories written for younger children, such as fairy tales and fantasy stories. What type of monsters are used in these stories? Make notes based on your discussion.

'The Selfish Giant'

'The Selfish Giant' by Oscar Wilde was written in 1888. It is a **fable**. These types of stories often contain some or all of these features:

- They are short prose texts.
- They are written in a simple style.
- They are written to entertain, but also contain a moral lesson.
- They are written for children, but the deeper ideas in them appeal to older readers too.
- They usually only have two or three characters.

Key word

fable: a short story designed to teach a moral lesson

- They contain fantasy elements, such as monsters or talking animals.

- Characters in them may be named for what they are (for example, King or Wolf) and defined by their name, attitude or power.

- The story usually has a happy ending.

- The ending reveals the moral message.

Read the first part of the story.

Extract 1

Every afternoon, as they were coming from school, the children used to go and play in the Giant's garden.

It was a large lovely garden, with soft green grass. Here and there over the grass stood beautiful flowers like stars, and there were twelve peach-trees that in the spring-time broke out into delicate blossoms of pink and pearl, and in the autumn bore rich fruit. The birds sat on the trees and sang so sweetly that the children used to stop their games in order to listen to them. 'How happy we are here!' they cried to each other.

One day the Giant came back. He had been to visit his friend the ogre, and had stayed with him for seven years. When he arrived he saw the children playing in the garden.

'What are you doing here?' he cried in a very gruff voice, and the children ran away.

'My own garden is my own garden,' said the Giant, 'any one can understand that, and I will allow nobody to play in it but myself.' So he built a high wall all round it, and put up a notice-board.

TRESPASSERS WILL BE PROSECUTED

He was a very selfish Giant.

The poor children had now nowhere to play. They tried to play on the road, but the road was very dusty and full of hard stones, and they did not like it. They used to wander round the high wall when their lessons were over, and talk about the beautiful garden inside.

'How happy we were there,' they said to each other.

prosecuted: taken to court for doing something illegal

1   Which features of fables can you identify so far? Compare your answers in small groups.

2   Fables often seem like simple stories, but they contain deeper meanings. These meanings are often represented by symbols. In your groups, discuss what the garden and the wall might symbolise in this story.

3   In this story, the **antagonist** and **eponymous character** is a giant – a monster figure. The writer uses different techniques to characterise the giant. Write a paragraph explaining how word choice, dialogue and the narrator's descriptions are used to present this character. Now read the next part of the story. As you read, see if you can identify the symbols.

> **Key words**
>
> **antagonist:** a character who creates problems in a story; a 'bad' character who stands in the way of the hero
>
> **eponymous character:** the character whose name is in the title of the story

Extract 2

Then the Spring came, and all over the country there were little blossoms and little birds. Only in the garden of the Selfish Giant it was still Winter. The birds did not care to sing in it as there were no children, and the trees forgot to blossom. The only people who were pleased were the Snow and the Frost. 'Spring has forgotten this garden,' they cried, 'so we will live here all the year round.' The Snow covered the grass with her great white cloak, and the Frost painted all the trees silver. Then they invited the North Wind to stay with them, and he came. He was wrapped in furs, and he roared all day about the garden, and blew the chimney-pots down.

'I cannot understand why the Spring is so late in coming,' said the Selfish Giant, as he sat at the window and looked out at his cold, white garden; 'I hope there will be a change in the weather.'

But the Spring never came, nor the Summer. The Autumn gave golden fruit to every garden, but to the Giant's garden she gave none. 'He is too selfish,' she said. So it was always Winter there, and the North Wind, and the Frost, and the Snow danced about through the trees.

One morning the Giant was lying awake in bed when he heard some lovely music. It sounded so sweet to his ears that he thought it must be the King's musicians passing by. It was really only a little linnet singing outside his window, but it was so long since he had heard a bird sing in his garden that it seemed to him to be the most beautiful music in the world. 'I believe the Spring has come at last,' said the Giant; and he jumped out of bed and looked out.

What did he see?

4 In groups:

    a   list the examples of personification in this extract

    b   discuss what the seasons, fruit and music might symbolise.

5 The writer's language choices help to make this seem like a simple story. For example, in this story, the writer uses mainly coordinating conjunctions ('and', 'but', 'or'). What does this tell you about the sentence types? What overall effect does it have in the story?

6 Stories written for children are usually clear and straightforward. Young readers need to understand what is happening in the plot and when it happens.

Look at the sentence openings in this extract. How many contain a **time connective** or a noun? Write a paragraph analysing how the writer uses connectives and sentence openings. Explain how they help the reader make connections in the story.

Self-assessment

What have you learnt about 'The Selfish Giant' so far? Make a list of brief details about:

- the plot
- the characters
- the way it is written.

Summary checklist

☐ I can identify and explain the key features of fables.

☐ I can explain the methods that writers use to present characters.

☐ I can identify symbols and personification in a text and comment on their effects.

☐ I can analyse how time connectives and sentence openings help structure a story.

Speaking tip

In group discussions, remember to ask questions and explore everyone's ideas. You might disagree with someone's interpretation when you first hear it, but it is important to give them a chance to explain their ideas, using evidence from the text.

Key words

time connective: a word or phrase used to show how events in a story are sequenced and linked by time – for example, 'then', 'next', 'before', 'after'

> 6.4 The little boy

In this session, you will:

- explore the effect of introducing a new character into a story
- trace a character's personal 'journey'
- discuss different interpretations of a story
- write your own fable.

Getting started

In pairs, remind yourselves of what has happened in 'The Selfish Giant' so far. Make some predictions about what will happen next. What do you think the giant sees as he looks out?

The next part of 'The Selfish Giant' introduces a **secondary character** who has an effect on the giant.

Key words

secondary character: a supporting character in a story; not the main character

Extract 3

In every tree that he could see there was a little child. The birds were flying about and twittering with delight, and the flowers were looking up through the green grass and laughing. It was a lovely scene, only in one corner it was still Winter. It was the farthest corner of the garden, and in it was standing a little boy. He was so small that he could not reach up to the branches of the tree, and he was wandering all round it, crying.

And the Giant's heart melted as he looked out. 'How selfish I have been!' he said; 'now I know why the Spring would not come here. I will put that poor little boy on the top of the tree, and then I will knock down the wall, and my garden shall be the children's playground for ever and ever.' He was really very sorry for what he had done.

So he **crept** downstairs and opened the front door quite softly, and went out into the garden. But when the children saw him they were so frightened that they all ran away, and the

crept: walked quietly

garden became Winter again. Only the little boy did not run, for his eyes were so full of tears that he did not see the Giant coming. And the Giant stole up behind him and took him gently in his hand, and put him up into the tree. And the tree broke at once into **blossom**, and the birds came and sang on it. And the other children, when they saw that the Giant was not **wicked** any longer, came running back, and with them came the Spring. 'It is your garden now, little children,' said the Giant, and he took a great axe and knocked down the wall.

> **blossom:** flowers on a tree
> **wicked:** mean and angry

1   In pairs, discuss the effect of the writer introducing this character: what impact does the little boy have on the Giant?

2   Stories often take characters on a journey of self-discovery, where they learn something important and change for the better because of it. The writer shows this change in the Giant through language choices. For example, at the start of the second paragraph we learn that *the Giant's heart melted*. The figurative use of the past tense verb *melted* suggests a change in the state of the giant's feelings.

Reread the story so far, then write a paragraph commenting on any other language choices that show the Giant's development. Use quotations in your answer.

Now read the final part of the story.

Extract 4

All day long they played, and in the evening they came to the Giant to **bid him** goodbye.

'But where is your little companion?' he said: 'the boy I put into the tree.'

'We don't know,' answered the children; 'he has gone away.'

'You must tell him to be sure and come here tomorrow,' said the Giant. But the children said that they did not know where he lived, and had never seen him before; and the Giant felt very sad.

The Giant was very kind to all the children, yet he **longed for** his first little friend, and often spoke of him. 'How I would like to see him!' he used to say.

Years went over, and the Giant grew very old and **feeble**. He could not play about any more, so he sat in a huge armchair,

> **bid him:** say
> **longed for:** missed or wished he could see
> **feeble:** weak

and watched the children at their games, and admired his garden. 'I have many beautiful flowers,' he said; 'but the children are the most beautiful flowers of all.'

One winter morning he looked out of his window as he was dressing. He did not hate the Winter now, for he knew that it was merely the Spring asleep, and that the flowers were resting.

Suddenly he rubbed his eyes in wonder, and looked and looked. It certainly was a marvellous sight. In the farthest corner of the garden was a tree quite covered with lovely white blossoms. Its branches were all golden, and silver fruit hung down from them, and underneath it stood the little boy he had loved.

Downstairs ran the Giant in great joy, and out into the garden. He **hastened** across the grass, and came near to the child.

And the child smiled on the Giant, and said to him, 'You let me play once in your garden, today you shall come with me to my garden.'

And when the children ran in that afternoon, they found the Giant lying dead under the tree, all covered with white blossoms.

hastened: moved quickly

3   Readers react to stories in various ways. On a simple level, you could express whether you enjoyed a story or not. On a more detailed level, you could discuss different interpretations of a story before deciding what you think of it. Here are three different readers' views about 'The Selfish Giant'.

In groups, discuss these views and find evidence in the text to support or challenge each one.

This is a story about people cooperating and accepting each other. The message is that the whole world needs to understand each other and work together.

This is a story reminding adults they have responsibilities – they have a duty to make the world a better place for future generations.

This is a story that suggests the purpose of life is to become the best and wisest human you can be.

Speaking tip

In group discussions, wait for your turn to speak, then make a clear point with some detail. Ask others whether they agree or not, to develop the discussion further.

4 You are going to write a short fable for children. Your fable should show one of these moral messages:

- appearances can be deceptive
- being honest is better than telling lies
- being patient (rather than rushing) leads to good outcomes.

Start by planning the basic plot of your fable and deciding which characters you will include. Remember that you must show events that lead to the moral you have chosen. Use simple language and some of the techniques you have learnt in this session and Session 6.3. Your finished fable should be approximately 200 words in length.

Peer assessment

Swap books with a partner. Read their fable and then:
- check that their story conveys a moral message
- tell them which part of the fable you enjoyed most and which part they could improve.

> 6.5 A smaller monster

In this session, you will:

- read a poem aloud
- explore a poet's methods of characterisation
- compare the techniques two poets use to explore a similar theme.

Getting started

In this session you will compare two poems about a smaller type of monster – a scorpion. Think of books and films you know that feature small animals. What different impressions of these characters are created? Are they comic, frightening or impressive? Discuss your ideas in pairs.

'The Scorpion'

This poem by Hillaire Belloc presents a scorpion in a comic way. The poet achieves this effect through specific use of **rhythm** and **rhyme**.

> The Scorpion is as black as **soot**,
> He **dearly** loves to bite;
> He is a most unpleasant **brute**
> To find in bed at night.

Key words

rhythm: a regular, repeating pattern of sound or 'beat', common in music and poetry

rhyme: words where the end part sounds the same (for example, 'feet' rhymes with 'meat')

soot: a black powder

dearly: greatly, very much

brute: a cruel person or animal

1   In pairs, take turns reading 'The Scorpion' aloud.

    In your reading, try to bring out the rhythm of the poem.

2   What language techniques does the writer use to characterise the scorpion? Write a paragraph explaining the impact of these techniques.

    You could consider the use of:

    • similes

    • specific verbs and adverbs

    • specific adjectives and **comparative adjectives**.

'Shadow of the Scorpion'

The second poem is set in an unnamed village. The narrator describes the dramatic events of a night when a scorpion enters the family home. The poem focuses on the reactions of the family members. The events of the evening are recounted in **chronological order**.

It crawled in front of the lamp,
A huge shadow cast on the wall, flickering
like a monster
in an old film.
We sat, **paralysed**.

Then it scuttled away somewhere, silently.

It was a long night **seared** in the memory of our family.
My mother, using a broom to search into dark corners,
My father, scared
but joking – playing the brave man we all needed.
My sister and me, frightened, strangely excited.

It struck in the night. My sister screaming. Her hand,
numb and swollen.

paralysed: unable to move
seared: burned

It was a long night seared in the memory of our family.

My mother, weeping and praying

My father, scared

but playing the brave man we all needed.

My sister, feverish, mumbling, struggling to breathe.

Me, frightened, desperate for her to survive.

As the sun rose, she was sitting up, smiling weakly.

Years later, I found out scorpion bites are unlikely to kill,

But the night still **casts a long shadow**.

> **casts a long shadow:** a metaphor meaning to have a long-term effect and to be remembered vividly

3   Draw a ten-part storyboard showing the main events of the story in the poem. Before you start, think carefully about which are the ten most important parts of the story. Beneath each part of the storyboard, make brief notes commenting on how the ideas and viewpoints have developed at each point.

4   One of the themes of the poem is about how humans react to – and remember – difficult situations. In pairs, look at the ways in which the family members react to the scorpion's attack and discuss what the poem shows about the way humans handle difficult situations.

5   You are now going to analyse how similar themes are presented in the two poems. Read the task:

> Compare the way scorpions and human reactions to them are presented in 'The Scorpion' and 'Shadow of the Scorpion'.
>
> In your answer, you should comment on:
>
> •   how scorpions are presented in both poems
>
> •   how the poets present human attitudes and reactions to the scorpions.

Start by planning your answer. Copy and complete the table on the next page in your notebook.

Poem	Scorpions	Human attitudes and reactions
'The Scorpion'	• seen as threatening and aggressive • suggests the scorpion enjoys causing pain (*dearly loves to bite*) • turns up unexpectedly • causes a sense of fear.	
'Shadow of the Scorpion'		• seen as mysterious and frightening – the simile *like a monster* suggests the fear it inspires • figurative term *paralysed* shows physical and emotional reaction • different characters show different reactions • sister's pain (*feverish*) • ending suggests long-lasting nature of human attitude.

Now write your response to the task, using your completed table to help you. Make sure your phrasing makes clear and logical sense, your spelling is accurate, and your handwriting is fluent. Write about 200 words.

Writing tip

A comparison can be structured in two ways. You could spend half of your response on one text in detail before comparing it to the second text, or you could regularly alternate between the two texts. Whichever way you choose, make sure it allows you to develop your points in detail.

Self-assessment

Read through your response. Check that:
- you have made comparisons between the poems
- you have included comments on the most significant features of language
- your phrasing makes clear sense.

❯ 6.6 Monster below ground

In this session, you will:

- read and respond to an informative article
- consider the use and impact of extended metaphors
- listen to and make notes on a description
- write an account using an extended metaphor.

Getting started

In pairs, write a definition of the term 'metaphor', giving some examples. Then discuss what the term 'extended metaphor' might mean.

Monster fatbergs

You are now going to find out about another monster. Although, this one is different – it is huge and found below ground, but this monster does not live and breathe.

Read this newspaper article by Chris Baynes, whose purpose is to inform people about 'fatbergs': giant lumps of fat that collect in sewers.

Monster fatbergs weighing more than 100 tonnes cleared from London sewers

Two 'monster' fatbergs as heavy as eight double-decker buses have been cleared from **sewers** in central London.

Engineers armed with power tools tackled the greasy giants – weighing a combined 103 tonnes – due to fears they could flood homes and businesses.

Thames Water said one 63-tonne fatberg, which included several tonnes of concrete, was cleared from a sewer close to Buckingham Palace.

Another **colossal** 70 m **clump** of fat, oil and grease was removed from the sewers near **the Shard**, in London Bridge.

The two fatbergs were blocking drains and threatening to **spew** wastewater into nearby properties the water supplier said.

Fatbergs are formed when fat and oil are poured down sinks and drains and stick to items that should not be flushed down the toilet.

Engineers use tools to break up the lumps before removing **chunks** by hand.

'It's an extremely difficult job getting them out of our sewers. It's hot and very unpleasant, especially when a chunk of fatberg is disturbed. The smell can be overpowering,' said Stephen Pattenden, network manager at Thames Water.

The water company said the two recent discoveries served as a timely reminder about the importance of properly disposing of cooking fat. It urged people not to 'feed the fatberg' and to take care of how they dispose of cooking fat.

Mr Pattenden said: 'Fatbergs are like monsters from the deep, lurking and growing under our feet, and the team worked **around the clock** to defeat these two before they could cause damage to our customers or the environment.

'We've all seen the problems and damage they cause, and I'd therefore ask everyone to please make sure they don't pour fats and oils down the sink.

'By letting the fat cool, putting it in a proper container like a glass jar and then in the bin stops a fatberg growing into a monster.'

sewers: underground pipes that carry waste water

colossal: very big

clump: a compact mass

the Shard: a well-known tall building in London

spew: to force out in large quantities

chunks: thick, solid pieces

around the clock: all day and night

1   In pairs, discuss your reactions to the article. Consider:

   •   how the details about fatbergs made you feel

   •   whether you would like to do Mr Pattenden's job.

Language focus

An **extended metaphor** is a comparison that is used and developed throughout a piece of writing. The metaphor adds layers to build up a dramatic picture of an event or character. For example, a simple metaphor might compare a sly character to a snake. An extended metaphor would make the comparison central to the whole description:

•   He slithered into the room slowly and silently, looking for his next victim. His narrow, beady eyes took in their surroundings and his head moved slowly from side to side, trying to catch sight of his prey. Once he found what he was looking for, he coiled himself on a chair and sat still, waiting to strike.

Notice how the features of a snake are used several times in this description. The writer extends the metaphor to emphasise the man's sly, threatening nature.

Key words

extended metaphor: a figurative language comparison that is developed throughout a piece of writing

---

2   In newspaper articles, journalists often present situations in a sensationalised way. This means that they exaggerate descriptions to make them sound dramatic, to attract and maintain the reader's interest. In this article, the writer uses an extended metaphor to present the fatberg as a monster. This helps the writer convey the fatberg's large size and makes the situation sound alarming and exciting to readers.

   Read the article again, noting down how the fatbergs are presented as monsters. Write a paragraph explaining the effect of this extended metaphor, using examples from the text.

 3   Later in this session, you are going to write imaginatively about fatbergs. To do so, you will need to gather some background information.

   Listen to a man called Bill Hall talking about his experience with fatbergs. As you listen, take notes on how it feels to confront a fatberg and the sensation of working in a sewer.

Listening tip

Where possible, listen to spoken texts several times. The first time, you should try to get a sense of the overall points and messages. On the second listen, focus on the smaller details.

---

4 Before you write your own account of a fatberg, read the opening part of a learner's response to the task. In pairs, identify the techniques the learner has used, including the use of extended metaphor and different sentence types. Which features do you think are the most useful in helping you imagine the fatberg and the writer's feelings?

> ## Meeting with a monster
>
> I looked into the small, dark opening in the road and knew what lay in wait. It was down there. Somewhere. Yes, down there – in the sewer – was a monster. It sat waiting in its lair, slowly growing bigger and blocking the tunnel, daring humans to try to pass it. Growling noises echoed along the tunnel as I lowered myself down the hole, switched my torch on and waded through the dirty water. This was it: a meeting with a monster. I knew what to expect. A faceless creature whose long legs stretched in both directions. Even though it had no eyes, I felt the monster watching me, desperate to drag me in and make me a part of itself.

5 Now, writing from the point of view of a worker, describe the process of going underground for the first time to confront a fatberg. Your writing should capture a mild sense of horror as well as the sights and sounds of the experience.

- Start by deciding on a metaphor that you can extend. You could use the idea of a monster or another idea of your own.

- As you draft your writing, remember to choose words that convey the sights, sounds and feelings of the sewer.

- Vary your sentences for effect and use any strategies you know to spell words correctly.

Self-assessment

Read your account again.

- How does your draft compare to the learner's answer?
- Which parts could you redraft to improve your response?

Summary checklist

☐ I can understand and explain the impact of information in an article.

☐ I can comment on the effect of extended metaphors.

☐ I can make effective notes to inform my own writing.

☐ I can plan and write an imaginative account using an extended metaphor.

Check your progress

Answer the following questions.

1 Explain what the term 'emotive language' means. Give examples from Session 6.1, Extracts 1 and 2.

2 What advice would you give about structuring an advice leaflet?

3 List some genre features of fables.

4 'The introduction of the little boy into the story has an effect on the giant'. Explain what this statement means in relation to 'The Selfish Giant'.

5 What advice would you give someone about the best way to compare two poems on similar themes?

6 What is an extended metaphor? Give an example.

Project

In this unit, the monsters you have read about have been defeated or problems associated with them overcome. Most books and films that feature monsters (or characters who act like monsters) usually end with the reassuring message that monsters can be defeated or changed.

In groups, you are going to research a range of books about monsters aimed at different audiences and try to find common patterns in these stories – not only the endings, but the settings, characters and events. Some monster stories you will have read, but there will be many that you will need to research. You can do this by reading plot summaries and study guides online.

Start by making a list of stories featuring monsters – for example, *A Monster Calls* by Patrick Ness and *Monster* by Frank Peretti. Then use the internet to help you extend the list. You should research:

- stories aimed at young children
- books written by international authors
- pre-20th century texts (such as *Frankenstein* by Mary Shelley).

Once you have concluded your research, find an interesting way to present your findings. This might be a large display poster, a presentation with images or a booklet.

7 'The Plantation'

In this unit, you will study 'The Plantation', a short story by Ovo Adagha. It is set in a small village in Nigeria and tells the story of Namidi, a worker on a rubber farm. You will explore how the writer uses the characters in the story, and the effects that the events described have on the reader.

> 7.1 The broken pipe

In this session, you will:

- give your impressions of setting, character and mood at the start of a story
- consider the use of imagery in creating an effective setting
- discuss and agree on a view about a character's actions
- write a diary entry from a character's point of view.

Getting started

In fiction, characters often make important decisions that affect what happens later in the story. In pairs, make a list of stories where characters make crucial decisions. What effect do these decisions have on the rest of the story?

'The Plantation'

Read the opening of this story by Ovo Adagha.

Extract 1

The plantation grew from the moist underbelly of the swamps. That place where greenery blocked away the sun and surrounded everything in sight; just as it surrounded Namidi that morning as he moved about to inspect his trees and traps. It was the *harmattan* season; the parching land breeze charged at him from the rubber trees and made the hairs on his skin bristle.

This place was an emblem of life to him – the high-pitched whistle of the birds; the cold drizzle of early morning dew; the rubber trees that glistened with sap. The plantation seemed to glow with a curious mysteriousness which followed him about as he moved **abstractedly**, slashing at the banners of plant-leaves that heaved across his path, his face a picture of dark **brooding**.

There followed a small moment of prickling silence, when it seemed as if the murmur of the plantation was suspended in a state of waiting. Namidi's nostrils picked up an odd, sickly smell that set his stomach on edge as he moved about; and with it floated an alien, trickling sound. He paused in mid-stride and **cocked his ears** at the trees. He stood still for a long time, listening, watching and sniffing, until, perhaps touched by an uncertain impulse, he looked behind a **thicket** a few feet away.

harmattan: a dry wind that blows over west Africa from the desert

abstractedly: lost in thought

brooding: deep in thought, possibly sad or angry

cocked his ears: turned his head to listen

thicket: a dense group of bushes or trees

1 Make notes on:

   a   your impression of the plantation as described in paragraph 1

   b   your impression of Namidi based on the information in paragraph 2

   c   how the writer creates tension in paragraph 3.

2 The writer combines language techniques to give nature unusual qualities in this extract. In pairs, make notes on how the writer describes the breeze and the plantation, identifying examples of:

   • aural, visual and tactile images

   • personification.

3 Write a paragraph explaining the overall impact of the techniques you explored in Activity 2. What impression of the natural world does the writer create? Use quotations to support your points.

Now read the next part of the story.

Extract 2

If the trees had started talking to him he would not have been more surprised. A stream of fluid burst forth from the ground and splashed all around. It flowed across the greenery, which seemed to shrink away. He watched as a puddle of fluid gathered around him and washed across the plantation. He realized it was petrol.

Once, many years ago, some men from the city in khaki uniforms had come to the village with long pipes and heavy trucks. They had dug across the village grounds, through the plantation and the nearby forests. A pipe must have broken, was the first thought that came to Namidi; he must ask the village head to do something about it.

But such noble thoughts soon evaporated as he turned the matter over in his mind. Yes, it was surely petrol, but of what benefit would this be to him? There was an opportunity here, if only the meddling of the villagers would let him. Then a small grin lit up his face. Yes, he knew what to do.

He filled the **rubber gourd** with some petrol and then started towards the village. When he emerged from the plantation the early morning sun was rising confidently in the skies. He walked on, scarcely responding to the greetings of the village women going to their farms. He, who usually lingered over greetings, now wished the women would all disappear and leave him alone.

rubber gourd: a kind of pot used to collect rubber from the rubber trees

4   At this point in the story, Namidi is faced with a choice – to report the leaking petrol or to keep his discovery a secret. Readers will react in different ways to the decision he makes.

In groups, discuss these three views, exploring the points you agree and disagree with. As a group, decide which of the three views you agree with most.

I can understand Namidi's decision. He probably doesn't have much money and when he finds the petrol, it seems like good luck. He's not stealing from anyone and it might make his life better.

I think he makes the wrong decision. He should have shared his discovery with the rest of the village. It might have made all of their lives richer and easier. Namidi acts selfishly.

Namidi is greedy and foolish. He is just interested in himself. The petrol spilling from the pipe could ruin the plantation. It could also be very dangerous and might harm the other villagers.

- How did your group come to its decision?
- Do you feel that the decision-making process was fair? Why or why not?

Speaking tip

When trying to reach decisions as a group, express your own ideas clearly and listen to everybody's contribution carefully. Discuss any ideas you agree or disagree with respectfully before making your decision. If you cannot all agree, take a vote to decide.

5   Imagine you are Namidi. Write a diary entry defending your decision. Try to make your explanation convincing.

You should explain:

- how you discovered the petrol

- why you kept your discovery secret.

Take care with your spelling, using any strategies you know in order to spell words accurately.

Summary checklist

- ☐ I can give my impression of setting, character and mood in the opening of a short story.
- ☐ I can comment on how a writer uses imagery to create an effective setting.
- ☐ I can contribute effectively to a group discussion and decision about a character's actions.
- ☐ I can write a diary entry showing the voice and viewpoint of a particular character.

› 7.2 Namidi's family

In this session, you will:

- identify explicit and implicit information and consider their effects

- explore the structural effect of introducing new characters

- consider how a reader's view of a character can change as the plot develops

- write imaginatively from a character's point of view.

Getting started

Stories usually contain secondary characters – those who are less important than the main character. In pairs, discuss stories you know that have memorable secondary characters. What sorts of things do these characters do? What do they add to the story?

In the next part of the story, the writer introduces a group of unnamed women. They do not play a significant role in the plot, but their presence allows the reader to find out more about Namidi's behaviour.

Extract 3

'Greetings, sir,' a group of women **rallied** at him.

'Greetings, good women,' he replied and hurried on without a glance in their direction.

'What is wrong with him?' one of them asked as they **appraised** the retreating figure. Namidi was moving briskly on the narrow path, his head thrust forward, like it was going to fall away from his neck.

'And he has this smell around him,' another one added.

'It smells like something they use with their rubber,' said another one. They stared at the departing figure and shook their heads in puzzlement.

Namidi moved as quickly as he could, his heart full of intent. Some riches are too hard won, he thought to himself, too long waited for to be shared, especially in this village where no man lacked greed and **treachery**. For long he had wandered and waited in the plantation for a chance to redeem himself from poverty. Now it was within his grasp to settle it. He would not share his discovery with anyone, he decided.

To avoid detection, he left the road and started walking off into the bush track: a steep, snaking slope of caked mud. He laboured up the path until he reached the village clearing; all the while nodding his head and whispering to himself.

> **rallied:** acted together in support of each other
>
> **appraised:** judged, considered the value of
>
> **treachery:** betrayal

1   Reread the extract and make notes on:

   • how Namidi reacts to the women and what this suggests about him

   • what the women think about Namidi.

2   At this point in the story, the writer reveals more about what Namidi is thinking. Write a paragraph explaining what the sentences *Some riches…from poverty* in Extract 3 tell us about his reasons for keeping his discovery of the petrol a secret.

Now read the next part of the story. Namidi returns home to his son, Ochuko, and his wife, Mama Efe.

Extract 4

The village itself was a cluster of thatched roofs. Namidi had lived there all his life and knew all about it: the small huts of red clay on a paltry piece of land with **minuscule** space between them; the rainfall and gossip that **ploughed on** endlessly; and how the very ground on which the village stood seemed swathed in a blanket of rust.

'Ochuko! Ochuko! Where in God's name is this boy?' Namidi called out when he got to his house.

'Papa!' a small, breathless voice rang out from behind the hut.

Namidi turned and regarded his six-year-old son as he came bouncing towards him from the backyard. Two years ago some **missionaries** had built a new school on the outskirts of the village. But the fees were expensive and he could not afford to send any of his three children there with the meagre earnings from his rubber farm. Namidi felt diminished each time he saw his boy playing in the sand.

'Go and call your mother for me,' he said.

'What is it?' his wife, Mama Efe, enquired as she emerged from the hut. She was a thin, shrivelled woman with a hardened look about her. Years and years of toiling in the sun had drawn the skin taut over her cheek-bones so that time and suffering seemed etched on her features.

---

minuscule: tiny

ploughed on: continued

missionaries: people on a religious mission to help a foreign country

---

Reading tip

When writing about structure in fiction, remember to consider the impact of key events or information in the story and when this information is disclosed. Ask yourself how they change the way you view a character or situation.

---

3   In this extract, the writer introduces two secondary characters – Namidi's wife and son. Look at the actions and dialogue of all three characters. In pairs, discuss:

- your impressions of Ochuko and Mama Efe

- your initial impression of Namidi's relationships with his wife and son.

4   In this part of the story, the description of the village and the introduction of other characters are key to the structure and the development of the plot. They help the reader understand more about Namidi and his situation.

Write a paragraph explaining:

- Namidi's feelings about his village
- how his inability to pay for school makes him feel
- how he might feel about his wife's 'suffering'.

5 In pairs, discuss whether this extract changes or confirms your previous view of Namidi's actions. For example, if you felt Namidi was selfish, does this part of the story encourage you to feel any pity or sympathy for him?

6 Look back at the diary entry you wrote from Namidi's point of view in Session 7.1. Now write a second entry in which you reflect on how you feel about your village, your six-year-old son and your wife.

Think about what voice would be appropriate for this diary entry, and consider Namidi's emotions. For example, perhaps Namidi is sad about his situation but optimistic for the future. Write 150 words.

Peer assessment

Swap your diary entry with a partner and assess how well they have responded to the task.

- Does the diary entry explore Namidi's feelings?
- Does the voice sound convincing?
- Are the spellings accurate?

Summary checklist

- ☐ I can identify and explain the impact of explicit and implicit information.
- ☐ I can comment on the structural effect of introducing new characters.
- ☐ I can explain how my view of a character changes as a story develops.
- ☐ I can write imaginatively, expressing a character's thoughts and emotions.

> 7.3 Namidi and Mama Efe

In this session, you will:

- explore how a writer presents the feelings of different characters
- consider the impact of a writer's structural choices
- write a monologue from a character's point of view
- perform a monologue using gesture and other non-verbal communication.

Getting started

In pairs, discuss any stories or films you know that feature families. In what ways are husband and wife relationships portrayed? What stereotypes of male and female behaviours are shown?

In the next part of the story, Mama Efe learns about the petrol.

Extract 5

'What's that smell you brought home today?' she asked, with a wary, suspicious frown on her face.

Namidi was gazing at his hut; at the lines of rotten bamboo that stuck out of its window panes. It seemed like the thatched roof and clay-red walls were **cowering** before him and the smell of new money. He turned around and told her about his findings.

'We must go there now before the **busybodies** get wind of it,' he added, trying to infect her with a sense of urgency.

'What if a fire starts, eh?' she queried, worriedly. In her mind, there appeared a flash of blurred images **writhing** inside a great flame; of **grotesque**-looking figures being planted in the ground; and of grey-clothed people standing around the fresh mounds of soil.

> **cowering:** crouching (in fear)
> **busybodies:** meddling, nosy people
> **writhing:** moving about as if in pain
> **grotesque:** ugly

Looking at her, at the doubt and anxiety that suddenly clouded her face, Namidi experienced a brief pang of fear; but he tossed the thought away quickly from his mind and said:

'It won't, I am the only one who knows.' His eyebrows arched menacingly, **admonishing** her to say no more.

She asked no further questions, but she thought within herself: this thing will come to no good.

> admonishing: reprimanding

1 Summarise Mama Efe's feelings about Namidi's discovery of the petrol. Use quotations in your summary.

2 The writer presents Namidi as a conflicted character. Part of him knows his actions are not right, but he continues with them anyway. Look at these lines, which show that Namidi is conflicted.

- *the thatched roof and clay-red walls were cowering before him and the smell of new money*

- *Namidi experienced a brief pang of fear; but he tossed the thought away quickly from his mind*

- *His eyebrows arched menacingly, admonishing her to say no more.*

In pairs, discuss:

a what these lines show about Namidi

b how you react to Namidi in this extract

c what you would do if you were in Mama Efe's position.

Now read the next part of the story, in which the whole family goes to collect the petrol.

Extract 6

Namidi, his wife and three children left the house with huge, empty cans. Namidi led the line, towering and frowning, as he **strode** determinedly down the bush path; his children followed, excited by the scent of adventure; his wife completed the moving line, her face brooding and disturbed. It was the road that would lead them to riches, he thought cheekily to himself. And as his wife and children trudged mechanically behind him, his mind was closed to all else except his destination.

> strode: walked quickly with long paces

Mama Efe cast a shadow on the ground as they worked their way back and forth from the plantation to the house, with large hauls of petrol. She followed him, without a word, saying nothing of the storm that was gathering in her heart.

Trouble lay in wait for them, she knew. Her heart throbbed with anxiety; yet not a word of complaint came from her. There was a time when she could have opposed him in some way, but long years of lost battles in her marriage had **doused** her spirits. Why, she knew how stubborn her husband could be; how he would never change his mind once it was made up. She used to think it was his strength. But she knew all about it now – all the ruin his **rigidness** had cast upon them.

> **doused:** put out (a fire or a light)
> **rigidness:** inability to change his mind or listen to other ideas

3 This is a key moment in the story structure – Namidi has involved his whole family in his secret. In pairs, discuss the effect of this plot device. Consider:

- what Namidi's children might know and feel
- what Mama Efe knows and feels
- whether your view of Namidi changes because of this event.

4 The writer builds up the character of Mama Efe in this extract, and allows the reader to see the situation from her point of view. Using details from the final paragraph, write a 150-word monologue from Mama Efe's point of view. Try to talk about:

- what you think is happening
- your feelings about Namidi
- what you anticipate might happen.

Start by skim reading Extracts 5 and 6 to remind yourself what is happening in this part of the story. Make notes on what you know about Mama Efe and what has come to light about her in the final paragraph. This will help you find the right voice to write your monologue. You could start:

I feel so helpless and angry. I'm so worried about what we are doing. It isn't right. I knew when Namidi came home smelling of petrol that something was wrong...

> **Writing tip**
>
> Monologues are meant to sound personal – almost like a confession. A monologue should contain information but also reveal feelings. When writing a monologue, imagine that you are speaking directly to one person.

5   In pairs, perform your monologue to each other. First, practise reading it aloud, thinking carefully about how you will perform it. Consider how you will use gesture and vary your voice to express emotion and make your meaning clear.

Peer assessment

In your pairs, give each other feedback on your monologues.

- What type of gestures did your partner use?
- What effect did they create?
- How did they vary their voice and how did this affect the performance?

Summary checklist

- [ ] I can identify how different characters feel and explain how a writer has conveyed those feelings.
- [ ] I can comment on the impact of a writer's structural choices.
- [ ] I can write a monologue in the voice of a character.
- [ ] I can perform a monologue using gesture and other non-verbal communication techniques to make my meaning clear.

Speaking tip

Pauses can be very effective when delivering monologues. They can signal to your listener that you are about to say something important. They can also give your listener time to think about something you have just said. When used effectively, pauses create a rhythm in your speech.

〉 7.4 Jackson and Ochuko

In this session, you will:

- consider the effect of introducing an antagonist into a story
- explore the use and impact of different types of adjective
- discuss the effect of descriptive language
- analyse the impact of a writer's structural choices.

Getting started

Many stories feature antagonists. How does this type of character usually behave? In pairs, think of some antagonists in stories you have read, and discuss their attitudes and actions.

The next part of the story introduces an antagonist, Jackson.

Extract 7

On the third trip to the plantation they were **accosted** by Jackson – a greasy-looking youth from the village. He was always up to no good and spent his days chasing birds and grasshoppers in the plantation. The lad took one sniff at Namidi and his eyebrows stretched wide.

'Why, are you working in **Shell** now?' he said, and grinned knowingly at Namidi.

Mama Efe was watching her husband as he eyed the youth with a look of hatred.

'What business of yours is it?' he **countered** in a cold voice, and surveyed the youth, like some **wayward** fly.

'You should know, anything that happens in this village I make it my business,' Jackson said, and rubbed his hands.

Namidi looked annoyed, like he had been insulted. He advanced towards the youth, eyes blazing, but held himself together with some effort when his wife placed a restraining arm on him. He turned away and continued walking, stiff-necked, down the narrow track. Mama Efe, a few steps behind her husband, was trembling with dread. He said not a word but she knew that darkness was brewing within him.

Already, the smell of the petrol had reached them; so too had the hissing sound from the plantation. Jackson uttered a cry behind them and then ran off in the opposite direction towards the village.

accosted: approached aggressively

Shell: an international oil company

countered: respond in a slightly hostile way

wayward: difficult to control, awkward

1   Reread the extract and make notes on:

- what Jackson says and does

- how Namidi reacts to Jackson

- how Mama Efe feels about the confrontation

- why the writer introduces Jackson into the story at this point.

Language focus

Adjectives are used to offer descriptive detail and indicate qualities in nouns. These include:

- opinion or measure: the *selfish* man, a *valuable* discovery

- size: a *big* problem

- shape: a *thin* woman

- age: a *young* man

- colour: a *green* forest

- origin: the *village* women

- material: the *metal* pipe

- qualifier (almost part of the noun): *the bush* path

If you are using more than one adjective, the order of qualities in this list is the order in which they should appear before the noun. For example:

The selfish, tall, old man stormed off.

opinion   size   age

---

2   The writer uses several adjectives in his description of Namidi, Jackson and their confrontation. The adjectives add detail to the sentence and help to characterise the two men. Copy and complete the table on the next page. You should identify the quality revealed by the adjective and analyse what it reveals about the situation.

Adjective	Quality	What it reveals
a **greasy-looking** youth (paragraph 1)	opinion	It shows Jackson's appearance and suggests he is unclean. It implies he has untrustworthy aspects.
he countered in a **cold** voice (paragraph 4)		
like some **wayward** fly (paragraph 4)		
a **restraining** arm (paragraph 6)		
walking, **stiff-necked**, down the narrow track (paragraph 6)		

Now read the next part of the story in which the whole village has discovered the petrol.

Extract 8

The day had progressed to a burning noon, with the sun gliding overhead like a circle of fire. Fishermen, farmers and women **swarmed** to the plantation, which seemed to glitter with a wave of sweat-drenched, dark bodies. All around, people fought each other for space around the site. Metal pans and buckets clashed and flashed in the **sweltering** heat like weapons of survival.

Namidi, his clothes dripping with perspiration and petrol, stationed Ochuko at an embankment, some distance away. He was to watch over the family possessions while his parents and siblings did their best at the pits.

But the boy wandered about and played with his friend, Onome. It was in their manner to climb a tree wherever they could find one. Up they climbed, laughing and swinging playfully from branch to branch, while the villagers below bubbled and brawled.

To the children, the fortune-hunters presented entertainment. They giggled at the sound of high-pitched voices drawn tight with tension; as grown men charged and shoved each other; as here and there a woman lost her footing, and rolled in a heap in the slimy soil.

> **swarmed:** moved quickly in a large group
> **sweltering:** extremely hot and humid

3   This part of the story is very descriptive. In pairs, discuss the overall impact of the vocabulary and language techniques the writer uses in the first paragraph. What mood do these choices create?

4   At this point in the story, the focus begins to shift to Ochuko. The writer structures the story to highlight the difference between how Ochuko feels about the dangerous situation unfolding at the plantation and how the adults feel about it.

Reread the extract and make notes on:

*   how the adults behave
*   how Ochuko behaves
*   what Ochuko does not understand about the situation.

5   What effect is created by Ochuko's lack of awareness about what is happening? Do you feel worried for him? Using details from the story, write a paragraph explaining the effect of the writer's structural choices in this part of the story.

> **Reading tip**
>
> Always consider the difference between what the reader knows and what the character knows. In some stories, readers can see that a character is making a mistake, or is heading for danger, even though the character can't. The impact of this can be a feeling of pity or fear.

Self-assessment

Read your paragraph and check that you have:
*   commented on the impact of the structure
*   used details from the story.

Summary checklist

☐ I can explain the effect of introducing an antagonist into a story.

☐ I can understand and explain the impact of different types of adjective.

☐ I can discuss how a writer's use of descriptive language establishes the tone of a scene.

☐ I can analyse the way a writer has chosen to structure part of a story.

> 7.5 The explosion

In this session, you will:

- predict how the story will end
- analyse how a writer uses language and structure to create specific effects
- have a group discussion about the ending of the story
- write an account of the events from a character's point of view.

Getting started

Stories can end happily, as the characters succeed, or sadly, as the characters suffer and fail. In pairs, note down some examples of stories that end happily and sadly. Which type of ending do you prefer and why?

1   In this session, you will read the last part of the story, in which an explosion occurs.

    a   How do you think the story will end?

    b   What will happen to Namidi and his family?

    c   Make a prediction and share it with the class.

- How did you make your prediction?
- What information in the story did you base your ideas on?

Now read the next part of the story. It starts with Ochuko and his friend playing in the trees.

Extract 9

Soon they were playing soldiers, their fingers serving as guns. Onome took aim at Ochuko and fired. And as Ochuko swerved to duck behind a branch, there was a flash of light and a deafening explosion that shook the tree he was hanging on. His young **adversary** fell from the tree, screamed and lay still.

Ochuko froze. There followed a brief moment when the world seemed **engulfed** in a blanket of yellow light. And then it broke loose with a yelling that rang out all at once. The boy stared at the growing **roost** of figures that broke out **frenziedly** from the smoky interior, running and swaying in scattered directions. He watched it all with a childish fascination.

But it was the heat that finally got to him – the hot, stifling sensation that suddenly seized him in a tight, airless embrace and threw him from the tree. In a flash, he was up on his feet and running off towards the village clearing. He ran, followed by the smell of burnt chicken feathers; by the long grasses and the screaming demons that leaped up and down behind him. The sky had turned grey and cast over him like nightfall. It made him run faster and faster towards the village and the familiar outlines of his father's hut.

Huge billows of smoke rose from the heart of the plantation as the dust-laden boy – his eyes itching with soot and tears – emerged from it. He ran into the hut and hid himself under his mother's bed.

> **adversary:** opponent
>
> **engulfed:** surrounded completely
>
> **roost:** a gathering (usually of birds, but used to describe people here)
>
> **frenziedly:** in an out of control way

2   In this extract, the writer combines features of language and structure to create a sense of both terror and pity. One key feature of structure is the use of contrast. In pairs, note down in your own words examples of:

- the contrast between innocence and danger

- the contrast between Ochuko's lack of understanding and the reader's understanding.

3 Write a 200-word analysis of how the writer creates feelings of terror and pity.

Focus on the use of contrast and techniques such as imagery and word choice. Use specific examples to illustrate your points.

Peer assessment

Swap books and read your partner's analysis.

- Have they written about a range of language and structural features, including contrast and types of imagery?
- Have they used quotations to illustrate their points?
- Have they explained how these examples create the overall effects of terror and pity?

Now read the last part of the story.

Extract 10

A little while later, after the sweat had dried from his body, he began to feel cold. He ventured to go outside, but then it was already dark. He heard the sound of running feet. Terrified, he whirled around and dived under the bed once again.

His were the pair of eyes that blinked and shone all night in the darkness. He tensed for a long time, listening for the sound of his mother's footsteps and the grating, angry thuds that were his father's. He waited and listened to the silence, occasionally broken by the distant wail of a woman crying, and the sound of feet running past the hut.

A small lamp – which his mother always kept alive – flickered and **petered out** as the night wore on. From the holes in the earth floor of the hut sprang a line of ants. It was their time of the night and, roused by the fresh smell of dried, oily sweat, they poured forth. He shivered in helpless immobility as their scrawny legs climbed across his back. He lay very still as they walked over him.

It was pitch dark for a long time. And even in the silence that followed, the boy waited and listened; but all he heard was the faraway bird-call of the coming dawn.

Writing tip

When writing an analysis, you can explain something in detail by examining the different techniques (for example, contrast, imagery and word choices) used. This will help explore how these contribute to the overall effect.

petered out: gradually got weaker, before going out

4   In small groups, discuss your reactions to the end of the story.
     Work through these prompts in sequence to help keep the
     discussion going. Remember to take turns and listen carefully to
     each other.

     •   Did the story end as you predicted?

     •   What emotions do you think Ochuko feels?

     •   What is the effect of ending the story by focusing
          on Ochuko?

5   Imagine you are Ochuko. You are now an adult looking back at
     what happened that day. Assume that you know about
     your father's actions and that the rest of your family
     died in the explosion.
     What do you remember and how do you feel?

     Write a 150-word account in which you explain:

     •   what happened in the plantation

     •   what you felt as you waited under the bed

     •   how you feel now as an adult.

     Start by using a suitable method of making
     notes from the extracts about the details of the
     explosion and by considering how an adult
     Ochuko might feel about his father's actions. Choose
     language precisely to express your thoughts. Use techniques such
     as figurative language. Use various strategies to help you spell
     words correctly.

Summary checklist

☐ I can use my understanding of a story to predict how it
   will end.

☐ I can analyse the language and structural techniques a writer
   uses to evoke particular responses from the reader.

☐ I can participate effectively in a group discussion about how
   a story ends.

☐ I can write an account exploring known events from
   a character's point of view.

> 7.6 Disaster reports

In this session, you will:

- write and perform a television news report
- listen to and evaluate a range of opinions about the story
- structure and write a formal report of an incident.

Getting started

Television news often contains reports from outside locations. How are these reports usually structured? In pairs, discuss how news reports begin and end.

1   In pairs, you are going to write and perform part of a television news report about the explosion at the plantation. Imagine that you are reporting the day after it happened and you are presenting from the scene of the explosion.

One of you will play the role of the reporter and the other will be Jackson, who has survived the explosion.

Use these prompts:

Reporter

Your role is to give facts about the explosion and find out some more details from Jackson. You should ask him about:

- the background to the explosion
- what he saw on the day of the explosion
- who might be to blame for the explosion.

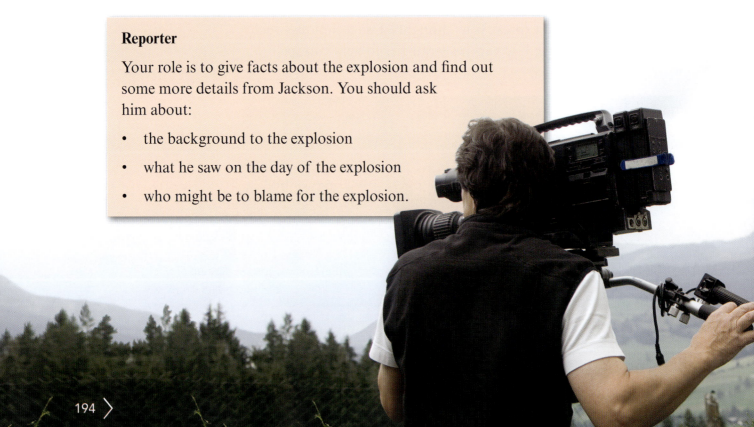

Jackson

Your role is to give an eyewitness account of the explosion. You should talk about:

- the build-up to it

- how it happened and what happened to you during and immediately after the explosion

- Namidi's actions.

News reports about dramatic incidents often follow a structure similar to this:

STORYBOARD

Scene: 01

The reporter speaks directly to the viewers, telling them where they are reporting from, briefly what happened and when.

Scene: 02

The reporter briefly introduces the eyewitness, explaining who they are and their relationship to the incident.

Scene: 03

The reporter asks the eyewitness to explain some facts and main points about the incident.

Scene: 04

The eyewitness gives an account of what they saw, usually starting with the most dramatic part.

Scene: 05

The reporter then asks the eyewitness more detailed questions about the background to the incident, the people involved and sometimes about feelings.

Scene: 06

The reporter finishes the report by summing up the outline of the incident.

Use this to help structure your own report. As you write it, think carefully about the language you use. Remember that the reporter will use clear but relatively formal English. As Jackson has probably never been interviewed on television before, he may speak more informally.

Writing tip

When you write a text that is meant to be spoken, you can make it seem more realistic by including some features of speech, such as discourse markers and pauses. However, make sure these features do not get in the way of communicating your character and ideas clearly.

2   Rehearse your report. Decide how much support you will need when you perform it and whether you want to read from your script or not. Think carefully about the characters you are playing and how you can use gesture and movement to express their personalities. Then perform your report, delivering your lines accurately and confidently.

Speaking tip

When performing a scripted report or scene, always keep in mind your audience and topic. Think how the listeners or viewers will react to your delivery. Make sure that your speech and movement is appropriate to the audience and the emotion of the situation.

3   When disasters happen, people search for reasons why. Listen to the audio track in which three learners give their opinion about the disaster. Make notes on each opinion.

4   Who do you think is to blame for the disaster? Work in pairs to consider all the opinions you heard, then write a paragraph together that summarises your findings. Make sure you use appropriate language to discuss this complex question.

Listening tip

When listening to opinions, always assess how well the person justifies their view. Listen carefully for evidence or detail to support the points the speaker is making, then double check these pieces of information.

Language focus

Using the **active voice** helps to make reports and other analytical writing clear. It shows who did what. Sentences written in the active voice often sound more direct and are easier for readers to understand. For example:

- Men from the city installed the pipe in the plantation.

The active voice shows the person or thing 'doing' the action (*Men*) before the verb (*installed*). The passive voice puts the person or thing after the verb:

- The pipe was installed in the plantation by men from the city.

The **passive voice** is also used in situations when it is not clear who did what:

- The pipe was installed in the plantation.

Key words

active voice: where the subject of a sentence is the person or thing performing the action

passive voice: where the verb comes before the person or thing, so the verb acts upon the subject

5 Public disasters like the one described at the end of 'The Plantation' are usually investigated by the police and other authorities. They generate reports that give factual accounts and suggest ways to avoid future disasters.

You are now going to plan and write a report into the explosion. Assume that the exact cause of the explosion has not been identified. Your report needs to decide who, if anyone, was to blame for the disaster.

At the end of the report, you will need to suggest any changes that need to happen in plantation areas. Your report should use the passive voice where appropriate.

Start your planning by looking back through the story and making notes on:

- why the pipe was in the plantation
- what Namidi's role was in the disaster
- who knew about the petrol
- why the explosion may have happened.

6 Now write your report, giving a balanced and accurate summary of what happened. Make sure you use language and structure suitable for a report. Remember that reports:

- use headings, subheadings and bullet points
- have introductions and conclusions
- are written in a factual tone – they avoid emotion
- use the active voice where possible
- use connectives to organise and link ideas
- use clear, precise language.

Summary checklist

☐ I can write and perform a television news report using an appropriate structure.

☐ I can listen to and evaluate a range of opinions about a story.

☐ I can use appropriate structural and language features to plan and write a formal report.

Check your progress

Answer the following questions.

1   Namidi decides to keep his discovery secret. Explain why this is a key moment in the story.

2   Namidi is poor. In your opinion does this explain his actions?

3   Describe the relationship between Namidi and Mama Efe.

4   List the eight different qualities that adjectives can describe.

5   Some readers think that Ochuko is the main victim in the story. Do you agree?

6   List the structural and language features of written reports.

Project

'The Plantation' explores ideas about human behaviour. It features a central character who makes a misguided decision and other characters who suffer because of it.

In groups, you are going to give a presentation about the story. Your presentation should focus on the following elements:

- the two main settings
- characters and their personalities and actions
- the themes of the story – poverty, greed, tragedy and suffering.

Be imaginative in the items you choose or make. You could draw or find pictures of the settings, make spider diagrams and images about the characters, and write short drama scripts. You could collect items that symbolise elements of the story or write brief paragraphs about the main themes. If you have access to technology, you could make a short film in which you explain aspects of the story. You could create an imaginative mime or dance performance of the main events, or even play a music playlist that captures the various feelings in the story.

Decide how your group will work best together – take up group roles that suit each member's skills. Once you have organised your ideas, present them to the class as confidently as you can.

8 > Choices and decisions

In this unit, you will explore how people make choices. You will read a short extract from a play by William Shakespeare, study a poem and article about choices and consider attitudes towards refugees.

> 8.1 *The Merchant of Venice*

In this session, you will:

- explore meanings, including moral lessons, in a play extract
- discuss different views of the play
- write and perform your own version of the extract.

Getting started

A riddle is a type of word puzzle. Riddles are like clues – they require the listener to think carefully and work out what is being described. Here is an example:

If you cut me, you will cry. What am I?

The answer is 'an onion'. In pairs, explain this answer. Can you think of any riddles of your own?

The Merchant of Venice

The part of this play by William Shakespeare that you are going to read features Portia, a rich single woman, and three men who want to marry her. Before Portia's father died, he made a rule that any man who wanted to marry Portia must be tested. In the test, each suitor (admirer) must choose one of three caskets (small boxes) that are made of gold, silver or lead. If the man makes the correct choice, he will marry Portia. Each casket contains a small roll of paper called a scroll. The correct casket also contains a picture of Portia. On the outside of each casket, there are riddles to help Portia's admirers choose:

Gold
Who chooses me shall gain what many men desire.

Silver
Who chooses me shall get as much as he deserves.

hazard: risk

Lead
Who chooses me must give and hazard all he has.

1 In pairs, read these messages and discuss:

- what the riddles might mean
- which casket you would choose if you were a suitor, explaining your choice.

2 In the three extracts on the next page, Portia's three suitors arrive to try the casket test. They are the Prince of Morocco, the Prince of Aragon and a young man named Bassanio. Bassanio truly loves Portia and she loves him.

Scan the extracts and note down:

- who chooses which casket
- which casket has Portia's picture inside.

▮ **Extract 1**

Enter Portia and the Prince of Morocco

MOROCCO But here an angel in a golden bed
Lies all within. **Deliver me** the key.
He unlocks the golden casket

There is a written scroll! I'll read the writing.

Reads

All that **glitters** is not gold;
Often have you heard that told.

> **deliver me:** give me
> **glitters:** sparkles

▮ **Extract 2**

Enter the Prince of Aragon

ARAGON … Well, but to my choice:
'Who chooses me shall get as much as he deserves.'
I will assume desert. Give me a key for this,
And instantly unlock my fortunes here.
He opens the silver casket

What's here? the portrait of a blinking idiot.

Reads

There be fools alive, **I wis**,
Silver'd o'er; and so was this.

> **I will assume desert:** I know what I deserve
> **I wis:** I know
> **silver'd o'er:** having silver hair

▮ **Extract 3**

Enter Bassanio

PORTIA I pray you, **tarry**: pause a day or two
Before you hazard; for, in choosing wrong,
I lose your company.

BASSANIO Let me choose
For as I am, I live upon **the rack**.

> **tarry:** take your time
> **the rack:** an instrument of torture

What find I here?

Opening the leaden casket

Fair Portia's **counterfeit**!

Here's the scroll.

Reads

You that choose not by the view,
Chance as fair and choose as true!

counterfeit:
picture

Fair Portia's counterfeit!

3 In groups of four, read all three extracts, taking one speaking part each. You should:

- read it slowly at first and help each other with difficult words and phrases

- use the glossary and other strategies to work out what is happening

- read it a second time, trying to pronounce the words as accurately as you can.

- What strategies did you use to work out difficult words and phrases?

- How might you improve this skill?

4 Each of the three suitors has a different attitude to the test. The Prince of Aragon thinks he deserves Portia – he says *I will assume desert*. The picture he sees and the words in the scroll suggest he is a fool.

What attitudes do the Prince of Morocco and Bassanio have towards the test? What lesson does the scroll teach them? Copy and complete the table on the next page.

Character	Attitude to the test	Moral lesson
Morocco	He thinks things that are worth the most money are the best. He chooses gold in the hope of improving his fortune.	The scroll tells him: *All that glitters is not gold.* This means …
Bassanio	He feels nervous that he might make the wrong choice.	The scroll tells him: *You that choose not by the view, / Chance as fair and choose as true!* This means …

5   Here are some views of this scene. In pairs, discuss the views and find some evidence from the extract to support them.

   a   It is clear that Portia wants Bassanio to succeed.

   b   Although the men have a choice, Portia does not.

   c   The extract shows that love is more important than money.

6   The Reduced Shakespeare Company is a group of actors who perform short, modern versions of Shakespeare's plays. In groups of four, write your own shorter, modern version of the scene from *The Merchant of Venice* (Extracts 1–3). Start by:

   •   deciding which are the most important lines in the scene

   •   rephrasing these lines in modern English.

Use the structure of drama scripts, including stage directions. Reduce your version to no more than 15 lines. You could start with:

MOROCCO: *Give me the key!*

7   Rehearse and then perform your script. Think about how you can use movement, gesture and your voice to bring your scene to life. Use the stage directions as a starting point, but vary your volume and tone. Remember to think about where you could use pauses.

Speaking tip

When performing in front of an audience, remember to emphasise movements and gestures. Use slightly exaggerated body language to help people watching understand the scene better.

> 8.2 Life choices

In this session, you will:

- work out the meaning of unfamiliar words
- consider implicit meanings in a poem
- explore how adverbs are used to show character and attitudes
- compare the ways different texts explore similar themes
- write your own thematic poem.

Getting started

Writers often explore similar ideas in their stories. In pairs, think of stories that focus on the same theme. What are the differences in the way writers explore these themes?

'The Road Not Taken'

In this poem by Robert Frost, the narrator describes a decision he makes while walking through a wood.

Two roads <u>diverged</u> in a yellow wood,
And sorry I could not travel both
And be one traveler, long I stood
And looked down one as far as I could
To where it bent in the <u>undergrowth</u>;

Then took the other, as just as <u>fair</u>,
And having perhaps the better claim,
Because it was grassy and wanted wear;
Though as for that the passing there
Had worn them really about the same,

And both that morning <u>equally</u> lay
In leaves no step had <u>trodden</u> black.
Oh, I kept the first for another day!
Yet knowing how <u>way</u> leads on to way,
I doubted if I should ever come back.

I shall be telling this with a sigh
Somewhere ages and ages <u>hence</u>:
Two roads diverged in a wood, and I—
I took the one less traveled by,
And that has made all the difference.

Note: This text uses American spellings.

1   Using your knowledge of word families and the context of the
    poem, write your own glossary to explain the underlined words.
    Use a dictionary to check you have understood the words correctly.

2   Many readers interpret 'The Road Not Taken' as a poem about the
    choices that humans make during the course of their life. The poem
    can be read as an extended metaphor for the important decisions
    we make.

    In pairs, discuss what the following lines suggest about the feelings
    associated with important choices.

    •   *long I stood*
        And looked down one as far as I could

    •   *knowing how way leads on to way,*
        I doubted if I should ever come back.

    •   *I took the one less traveled by,*
        And that has made all the difference.

'No Going Back'

Writers often use literal choices to represent important moments in life. Read this short story about a visit to a swimming pool which presents the idea of growing up.

Oliver had been here so many times. As a young boy, he'd stood in the water and looked up, totally in awe at the men diving from the board. As they **hurtled** down aggressively towards the water, they seemed like eagles, diving with their eyes rigidly fixed and their bodies **poised**. But today, almost without thinking about it, Oliver found himself steadily climbing the steps up to the diving board. His father was behind him. As he stood on the board, he looked back hesitantly. 'You can come back if you want,' said his father. Oliver paused. He wanted to, but some unknown force made him walk to the edge and dive. There was no going back.

> **hurtled:** moved very quickly
>
> **poised:** to be ready to do something

Language focus

Adverbs show how a verb action is being done. They can also modify an adjective to give more detail about the manner and extent of an action. Notice how the underlined adverbs in these sentences add detail:

- He <u>greedily</u> ate the food.
- She crept up the stairs <u>quietly</u>.
- I was <u>very</u> angry.
- I <u>almost</u> fell over.

Adverbs of manner tell you about *the way* something is done – for example, 'quickly', 'horribly', 'fast', 'thoughtfully', 'incorrectly'. Adverbs of degree tell you the *extent to which* something has happened – for example, 'completely', 'quite', 'very', 'totally', 'almost'. Choose adverbs carefully in your writing as they can say a lot about a character's attitudes and feelings.

3 'The Road Not Taken' and 'No Going Back' explore a similar theme – life choices. Compare the ways both writers present this theme. Start by making notes on:

- how the narrators feel about their choices

- key lines in each text

- the metaphors each writer uses

- the use and effect of adverbs

- structures such as rhyme, rhythm and sentence variety.

Once you have made your notes, write two paragraphs comparing the texts. Use quotations in your answer.

4 You are now going to write your own poem about choices and decisions. Your poem should use the same metaphor as 'No Going Back' – jumping off a diving board to represent growing up. Look again at the story and start by deciding if you will:

- use words or phrases from the story

- use rhyme in your poem (it may be easier not to).

Plan and draft your poem. You could do this in a number of ways – by starting with a title, by trying to write the final lines or by writing lines and phrases as they come to you. Once you have some ideas, experiment with the layout of your poem. You might try writing the poem in one **stanza** or several.

When you have finished drafting your poem, write it out neatly, taking care with your handwriting. Decide on a layout that suits the poem. For example, you could think about where to place the stanzas, the size of title, and whether you should add a picture.

> **Key word**
>
> stanza: a group of lines of poetry, forming a unit

> **Writing tip**
>
> Redraft your poem as many times as necessary to ensure you are happy with it. Cut lines that are not working, or try placing them elsewhere in the poem. Remember that the title and closing lines in a poem are usually the most important, so spend time on these.

Summary checklist

- [ ] I can work out what unfamiliar words mean using different strategies.
- [ ] I can identify and explain implicit meanings in a poem.
- [ ] I understand how adverbs can be used to add descriptive detail.
- [ ] I can compare the ways writers explore similar themes.
- [ ] I can plan and write a poem using a metaphor.

> 8.3 Making decisions

In this session, you will:

- listen to, discuss and evaluate ideas
- identify the main and subsidiary points in an article
- explore how writers use adverbs to link information
- write an account using appropriate structural devices.

Getting started

Both fiction and non-fiction feature characters or people who make important decisions. In pairs, discuss any stories you know where the plot includes a character having to make a significant choice about something. What are these decisions and how do the characters make them?

Listening tip

When listening to people's opinions, take time to fully evaluate what you hear. You could write a PMQ table showing the **P**lus points (things you agree with), **M**inus points (things you disagree with), and also a list of **Q**uestions – (things you need further information about).

1 How do people make decisions? Listen to the audio track in which various speakers give their advice about decision-making. Answer the questions below.

   a Why does Durjoy think that following your instincts results in good decisions?

   b Summarise Chaturi's advice.

   c What does Helmut think are the benefits and disadvantages of asking others for advice?

   d Evaluate the advice of the three speakers – which bits of advice do you think are most useful?

2 Look at this list of four suggestions for ways in which the world could be improved.

   - Rich people should share their wealth with poor people.
   - The whole world should stop eating meat.
   - Cars should be banned.
   - Children should start school at the age of eight.

In groups of four, discuss and evaluate these suggestions and make a decision on which of the four suggestions should be introduced. Talk about what you agree and disagree with.

Before you start, decide what roles each person might take in the group. For example, you might want to have a chairperson who keeps the discussion focused on the task, or a prompt person who asks questions to keep the discussion moving forwards. Finally, reach an agreement on which of the four suggestions should be introduced.

> Did people in your group take on different roles? If so, how did you decide who took on what role? If not, why not?

A choice problem

You are now going to read an article by Kate Douglas and Dan Jones that analyses decision-making. It describes research by scientists and suggests an unusual way to reach a decision.

97

Top 10 ways to make better decisions

We tend to believe that we will always be happier being in control than having someone else choose for us. Yet sometimes, no matter what the outcome of a decision, the actual process of making it can leave us feeling dissatisfied. Then it may be better to **relinquish** control.

Last year, Simona Botti from Cornell University and Ann McGill from the University of Chicago published a series of experiments that explore this idea. They asked volunteers to randomly select one item from a list of four. They later realised that two items were ones with pleasant smells (such as coffee or chocolate), and two were items with unpleasant smells. Once the choice was made they completed questionnaires to rate their levels of satisfaction with the outcome and to indicate how they felt about making the decision.

As you might expect, people given a choice of pleasant options tended to be very satisfied with the item they picked and happily took the credit for making a good decision. When the choice was between nasty options, though, dissatisfaction was **rife**: people did not like

> **Speaking tip**
>
> Deciding on roles before you begin a group discussion can help it run smoothly. One way to do this is to consider who has expertise in the subject being discussed, or who is good at asking key questions. Watching how others contribute is a good way to develop your own skills.

relinquish: to give up something
rife: very common

their choice, and what's more, they tended to blame themselves for ending up with something distasteful. They would have been happier not to choose at all.

Botti believes these findings have broad **implications** for any decision. Try letting someone else choose the restaurant, for example. You might also feel happier about leaving some decisions to a professional. Botti's latest work suggests that people prefer having a doctor make choices about which treatment they should have. 'There is a **fixation** with choice, a belief that it brings happiness,' she says. 'Sometimes it doesn't.'

> **implications:** conclusions that are not explicitly stated
>
> **fixation:** an obsession

3 Summarise the main points and the subsidiary information from paragraphs in the article. Use strategies such as skimming and scanning to do this. Use a table like this one to record the points.

Main points	Subsidiary information
• Volunteers asked to choose from four items. • Pleasant or nasty choice offered.	• Research conducted by Simona Botti from Cornell University and Ann McGill from University of Chicago.

Language focus

In writing that describes a sequence of events, gives contrasts or makes references to time, you can use specific adverbs to help the reader see connections.

The words underlined in the example here are **linking adverbs**. These help the reader see the stages in a scientist's career.

- It takes a long time to become a scientist. <u>First</u>, I had to study hard at school. <u>Next</u>, I went to university. <u>Afterwards</u>, I looked for a job near my home town.

The words underlined in the next example are **time adverbs**. These show the process of the scientist's work and allow the reader to see how stages link together over time.

- <u>Last year</u>, I decided to start some new research. <u>Recently</u>, I made a breakthrough. <u>Soon</u>, I will share my findings.

> **Key words**
>
> **linking adverb:** an adverb that shows a sequence in time or contrast (for example, 'afterwards')
>
> **time adverb:** an adverb that shows when something happens (for example, 'yesterday')

4   The article is carefully structured to help the reader understand the research it analyses. Each paragraph develops the information and sentence openings are used to link ideas within each paragraph.

   a   Summarise the function of each paragraph – what 'job' does it do in the overall article?

   b   Explain how linking adverbs and time adverbs are used to help the reader understand the stages of the experiment.

5   Write an account of an important decision you have made – perhaps related to friendships, sport or school. Explain:

   •   what choices were available to you

   •   how you made your decision (what process you went through)

   •   how you felt afterwards.

   Write 150 words and use time and linking adverbs to organise your writing.

Peer assessment

Swap books with a partner and check if:
- the three bullet points of the task have been addressed in full
- time and linking adverbs are used accurately.

Summary checklist

☐ I can participate in a group discussion, listening to and evaluating ideas.

☐ I can use different strategies to identify the main and secondary points in an article.

☐ I can understand how writers use adverbs to connect information.

☐ I can write an account using appropriate structural devices such as adverbs.

> 8.4 A dangerous decision

> **In this session, you will:**
>
> - use drama skills to show your understanding of a story
> - explore the structure of a newspaper report
> - analyse the content and grammatical structure of opening paragraphs
> - write some opening paragraphs for newspaper reports.

Getting started

Gesture and facial expression are effective ways of conveying emotions. On your own, write down five emotions. Then pair up and take it in turns to demonstrate the emotions on your list using only facial expressions, body language and gesture.

High-speed terror

This newspaper article by Bonnie Malkin reports a story in which a man puts his own life in danger by making a split-second decision.

Tourist feared he would die

An American tourist has told how he feared he would die as he spent two and a half hours clinging to the outside of a train travelling through the Australian **outback** at speeds of up to 70 mph.

Chad Vance, a 19-year-old student from Alaska, jumped on to the Ghan, which travels from Adelaide to Darwin, as it pulled out of Port Augusta. He had hopped off to stretch his legs during a stop, and panicked when he saw it moving off. He managed to squeeze into a small **stairwell**, but as the train gathered speed and night fell he realised his decision could be fatal.

'I was worried I wasn't going to survive,' he said. 'If I'd fallen off at that speed and hit the nasty-looking rocks below, I don't think I would have made it.' He clung on for two hours and 20 minutes before Marty Wells, a crew member, heard his cries for help and brought the train to an emergency stop. 'Chad is a very lucky guy. When we rescued him his skin was white and his lips were

outback: a remote area of Australia

stairwell: the outside part at the end of a train carriage housing some steps

blue,' Mr Wells told a newspaper. 'We were still about three hours away from our next scheduled stop and in that time he could have easily died of **hypothermia** or lost his grip.'

Mr Vance boarded the Ghan in Adelaide on 28 May for the journey to Alice Springs. He lost track of time in Port Augusta and arrived back at the platform as the train was moving off. He said he knew it would pull up outside to change drivers, so he decided to chase it. When he caught it up, he banged on the windows of the first-class dining carriage. The passengers ignored him because they 'probably thought I was some crazy kid,' he said.

After five minutes, the train started to pull away again and he made the 'instinctive' decision, which he admitted was a 'pretty crazy idea', to climb back on board. Wearing only jeans, boots and a T-shirt, he endured freezing temperatures before he was rescued.

'He was shaking uncontrollably for several hours and complained of numbness to the left side of his body and arms and said his face was also stinging,' Mr Wells said.

> **hypothermia:** a condition in which body temperature drops to a dangerously low level

1   In groups of four, **mime** the events described in the article. There are four roles:

- Chad Vance

- Marty Wells

- two passengers.

Mime each stage of the story, and use gesture and movement to convey the drama of the events.

2   In pairs, explore what this article shows about decision-making and its consequences. Discuss these questions:

- What reason does Chad give for jumping on the train?

- What does the story show about the way humans make decisions?

- What saves Chad from death?

3   The writer of this article tells the story in an unusual sequence. The first three paragraphs outline what happened after Chad jumped

> **Key word**
>
> **mime:** to act something out without words or sounds, using only body language, movement and gesture

back *on* the train at Port Augusta, up to the point where he was rescued. Look at how the last three paragraphs expand the story.

- Make notes on the extra details given.

- Explain why the writer might have chosen to structure the article in this way.

Language focus

Prepositional phrases add detail by showing the relationship between a noun and another word in a sentence. Prepositional phrases may consist of a **preposition** followed by a **noun phrase** or a pronoun. In these examples, the preposition is in bold and the noun phrase or pronoun is underlined:

- The passengers were tired **during** the train journey.
- He was yelling **at** me.

Prepositional phrases may also consist of a preposition followed by an adverb or an **adverbial phrase**. In these examples, the preposition is in bold and the adverb or adverb phrase is underlined:

- **From** there, you can travel to Adelaide.
- **Until** quite recently, I'd never been on a train.

Another type of prepositional phrase consists of a preposition followed by a prepositional phrase, like this:

- It would be better to wait **until** after the train stops.

Using a variety of these sentence structures to add detail can improve your writing and give your readers a good sense of when and how events occurred.

Key words

prepositional phrase: a group of words consisting of a preposition followed by a noun (or sometimes an adverb or another preposition)

preposition: a word or group of words used before a noun or pronoun to show place, direction, time, etc. (for example, 'above', 'below', 'under', 'in')

noun phrase: a phrase that contains a noun and describes the qualities of an object

adverbial phrase: a word or phrase that adds detail or information to a verb

4   Newspaper articles aim to establish the key facts of a story in the opening paragraph, which often consists of a single sentence. They usually briefly tell the reader who the story is about, what happens and where it happens.

In pairs, analyse the grammatical structure of the opening paragraph of the article 'Tourist feared he would die'. Explore:

- where the nouns are placed, especially the main person in the story

- the verbs used and how they suggest danger

- the use of prepositional phrases to add detail.

5   Write some paragraphs that briefly but clearly give the reader key facts about different stories. Use prepositional phrases to add details. Use these three ideas as starting points:

- a diver who finds some treasure

- a sports team that wins an important game

- an accident at a train station.

Self-assessment

Read your three opening paragraphs.

- Have you given key details about the story in a clear way?

- How could you make the details even clearer?

- Have you used prepositional phrases accurately to add detail?

Summary checklist

- ☐ I can mime the events of a newspaper article to show my understanding through performance.
- ☐ I can comment on the structural features of a newspaper report.
- ☐ I can analyse the effect of opening paragraphs, considering content and structure.
- ☐ I can write my own effective opening paragraphs for newspaper reports.

Reading tip

When working out word classes in a sentence, start by identifying the verbs (remember that words like 'is' and 'was' are verbs) as they are the 'muscle' of a sentence. Next, identify the nouns – the people and things 'doing' the action of the verb. Remember that dictionaries will classify the grammatical class of words, so use them to help you when needed.

> 8.5 Impossible choices

In this session, you will:

- read and understand a text about people in difficult circumstances
- explore the use and effect of language and structure to persuade
- discuss and decide whether a text is biased
- write a personal response to a persuasive text.

Getting started

News reports sometimes feature people in very difficult situations. In pairs, discuss any news reports you might have seen or heard. What was the difficult situation? How did you feel when hearing about these people?

To be a refugee is to make impossible choices

The following blog recounts the experiences of refugees. It was written by Elizabeth Olson, a worker for the charity Oxfam. The blog informs people about what life is like for refugees, but its main purpose is to subtly persuade readers to view refugees sympathetically.

When was the last time you had to make an impossible choice?

In late May, Oxfam hosted The Refugee Road, an event which involved researching refugees and their stories. One story in particular that continues to haunt me is that of Ahmad Mohmammad and his family. He, his wife and five daughters fled their home in Homs, Syria in 2013 after his 9-year-old daughter was shot. At the time this story was recorded, his family was living in a cramped apartment in Zarka, Jordan and was considering making the journey across the Mediterranean. Ahmad himself has been shot at three separate times and has witnessed the murders of many others. He states, 'I'm willing to take the risk and face the danger of travelling to Europe if it will help my children have a better life.'

Many of the refugees whose stories I observed said something similar – that they were willing to take the risk, that they felt they had no choice. One woman, Doaa, couldn't simply go back to Syria – her father's business had been **decimated** in an explosion and her family had nothing left. She and her boyfriend decided to risk giving their entire life savings to **human traffickers** who offered to take them. Ultimately, Doaa and a handful of others made it across the Mediterranean, but the other 500 passengers **perished** when the boat sank after being attacked by pirates.

Had she been aware of her fate on that boat, Doaa wouldn't have chosen to take it. But she had to make an impossible choice: remain and fear for her life every day, or risk it all in pursuit of a stable living situation in northern Europe. Either of those choices could have led to an **unspeakable** fate.

Refugees are simply people who drew the wrong ticket in the game of life. It's easy to distance yourself from a refugee if you haven't lived through a war, but the reality is that there's no guarantee you'll never be a refugee yourself.

> **decimated:** seriously damaged or destroyed
>
> **human traffickers:** people who illegally transport other people between countries
>
> **perished:** died
>
> **unspeakable:** too horrific to talk about

1   Answer the following questions.

   a   Explain what happened to Ahmad Mohmammad and his family. Why is he willing to travel to Europe?

   b   Summarise Doaa's experience. What does the writer mean when she says *Either of those choices could have led to an unspeakable fate*?

   c   What is your initial reaction to this blog?

2   In the final paragraph, the writer uses *the game of life* as a metaphor to describe refugees' experiences. Explain what this comparison means. What is the writer suggesting about who is to blame?

3   The purpose of the blog is to persuade people to help refugees, but the persuasive techniques that the writer uses are quite subtle. Remind yourself of common features of persuasive writing:

hyperbole   rhetorical questions   exclamations   statistics   emotive language

repetition   figurative language   direct address   imperatives   triples

In pairs:

a Identify which of these techniques are used, noting down where they occur in the structure of the text and their impact. For example, you might note that the figurative use of *haunt me* occurs before the story of Ahmad is introduced, which leads the reader to see the story as distressing.

b Discuss the impact on the reader of using refugees' personal experiences as the main focus of the blog.

4 Any text that presents only one view of a situation may be accused of bias. This is especially true of persuasive texts. Here is the Cambridge Dictionary definition of bias:

The action of supporting or opposing a particular person or thing in an unfair way, because of allowing personal opinions to influence your judgement.

In pairs, discuss whether or not the blog about refugees is biased. Start by considering the reasons for writing the blog and the way language is used. Do you and your partner agree on whether or not it is biased? If you do feel it is biased, what do you think is the impact of this bias on the reader?

5 Write a personal response to the blog, explaining how you react to the information it contains and the way the writer has presented it. You should write about:

- whether the stories of Ahmad and Doaa affected you

- whether you agree with the writer's points about human choices

- how the language and structure of the blog might have influenced you.

Write 150 words. Choose your words carefully in order to precisely express your views.

> **Writing tip**
>
> When giving a personal response, remember to focus mainly on your own views, feelings and attitudes. Personal responses often explore how a text affects a reader, so start by thinking what emotional reaction you feel to what you have read.

- What were the challenges of expressing a personal response?
- How did you try to overcome them?

Summary checklist

- ☐ I can explain explicit and implicit meanings and their effect in a persuasive text.
- ☐ I can identify persuasive features and comment on their effect.
- ☐ I can decide whether a text is biased or not and explore the effects of bias.
- ☐ I can write an effective personal response to a persuasive text.

〉 8.6 Different views

In this session, you will:

- use a range of strategies to work out the meaning of unfamiliar words
- explore the content and structure of an argumentative text
- compare and discuss viewpoints in different texts on the same theme
- plan and write an argument text.

Getting started

In pairs, make a list of the strategies you have learnt to work out the meaning of unfamiliar words. Discuss which ones you use most and why.

Do developed countries have a responsibility to welcome refugees?

This article by Norashikin Mohamad presents a view about refugees, using some words and phrases that you may not be familiar with. Before reading the article, work in pairs to find out the meaning of the underlined words and phrases. Use a range of strategies to do this. Then read the article.

The refugee question

The current situation brought about by the movement of refugees seeking safe and secure homes in <u>developed countries</u> **brings to the fore** that one question – do developed countries have a responsibility to welcome refugees?

Developed countries should <u>prioritise</u> and meet the needs of their people first, to the best of their abilities. For instance, the availability of food, housing and medical care should meet the requirements of the people in the developed countries. The presence of refugees in developed countries may bring with it challenges, one of which is the pressure to provide housing, food and medical care to the refugees. Some developed countries such as Germany and France are already facing a shortage of resources in areas such as housing. The arrival of refugees threatens to worsen the problems that are already present in these developed countries.

Moreover, refugees bring with them a different way of life from that which has already been <u>established</u> in developed countries. Refugees often suddenly arrive with little understanding of the new environment. They come with different values, beliefs and cultures, and these threaten to **disrupt the stability** of developed countries.

While it is true that more successful developed countries should aid fellow human beings who are in <u>urgent</u> need of help, welcoming refugees to their countries is not the most effective <u>mode</u> of help. For example, 1 in 40 people die attempting to sail from Libya to the Mediterranean Coast. Even if they survive the journey, refugees are often housed in camps which are ill-equipped, resulting in refugee families contracting diseases, **worsening their plight**.

It is best that the efforts in helping the refugees be channelled towards helping them rebuild their own countries rather than depending on developed countries.

brings to the fore: raises

disrupt the stability: make a situation less secure or successful

worsening their plight: make a bad situation worse

1   In pairs, discuss your initial response to the argument. Do you agree with the writer? Why, or why not?

2   Argumentative articles are usually structured as a series of points in a logical sequence. What are the main points of the argument in this article?

    a Look at paragraphs 2, 3 and 4 and identify the three main ideas presented in them.

    b Consider the purpose of the opening and closing paragraphs. How do they help to shape the argument?

3   The article in this session and the blog 'To be a refugee is to make impossible choices' from Session 8.5 present different views on the same topic. Briefly summarise the views and purposes of both texts.

4   The writer uses a variety of techniques to organise and present her argument:

- a paragraph introducing the topic
- a rhetorical question
- **topic sentences**
- modal verbs
- examples from real life
- a connective to introduce another point
- an acknowledgment of the other side of the argument
- a concluding remark to summarise the main idea.

Identify each of these techniques in the article. Compare your answers with a partner and discuss the overall impact of these techniques on the reader.

5   You are going to write an article arguing that developed countries should accept refugees. Focus on presenting your ideas in a clear, structured way, using some of the techniques you have explored here and in Session 8.5.

Begin by doing some research into facts about refugees. You could use some material from the blog in Session 8.5 as well as other sources. If you can, find other argumentative articles and look at the way language is used.

Writing tip

When summarising a text, begin by stating its purpose and then give the main view or idea it contains. Look at the opening and closing paragraphs, as these often provide a summary of the text.

Key words

topic sentence: a sentence that expresses the main idea of the paragraph in which it appears

Plan your work. Use a list or spider diagram to generate ideas. Then organise your ideas into a logical sequence. Write 200 words and use standard English to help you create a sense of formality.

Self-assessment

- Read your work and check that you have presented your points in an effective sequence. Do the opening and closing sections shape the argument and help the reader to grasp the overall view?

- Are the points presented in a logical sequence – do they build on each other?

Summary checklist

- [ ] I can use a range of strategies to work out the meaning of unfamiliar words.
- [ ] I can comment on the content and structure of an argumentative text.
- [ ] I can compare different viewpoints on the same topic and express a personal response opinion.
- [ ] I can plan and write an argument text using a clear structure.

Check your progress

Answer these questions.

1   Give three ways you can perform a drama scene to really bring it to life.

2   Give definitions of the terms 'manner adverb' and 'degree adverb', using examples.

3   Give definitions of the terms 'linking adverb' and 'time adverb', using examples.

4   Describe the structure of an opening paragraph of a newspaper report, including grammatical patterns.

5   Explain the possible impact of bias on a reader using an example.

6   List techniques that can be used to organise and present an argument.

Project

Your class is going to hold a competition called Book of the Century. In groups of four, play the role of a publishing company. You must choose and then promote a book and persuade people that your book choice should win Book of the Century. Voting will decide the winner.

In your groups, choose a book you think will appeal to people your age, avoiding well-known titles. Then, find out all you can about the plot, character and themes of the book. Read the opening chapter, the blurb and research the author.

Write a sales pitch and make the book sound as appealing as possible, citing reasons why you think it deserves to win. Use some visual aids, such as a copy of the book cover or pictures to represent the action of the book.

In the presentation, each member of the group should speak about an aspect of the book – plan carefully. You might like to use visual aids. Remember that you are trying to convince your listeners that your book is the best, so be as persuasive as you can.

Once presentations are complete, have a class vote to decide which book wins. Include a small prize for the winning company!

9 ▶ Endings

In this unit, you will study endings – moments where people's lives change and they enter a new phase. You will read accounts and poems written by parents, and a text in which someone looks back at their childhood. You will also explore the ending of a story you read earlier in this book.

> 9.1 Saying goodbye

In this session, you will:

- consider implied meaning in a descriptive account
- explore the meanings of a range of metaphors
- consider the use and effect of conjunctions
- explore your own and other people's responses to a text.

Getting started

In life, there are times when things come to an end – for example, at some point in their life everyone leaves school and leaves home. These endings cause a mixture of emotions. In pairs, talk about a time when you changed schools or moved to a different class. Discuss:

- what you can remember and how you felt
- how your parents or guardians might have felt about it.

Leaving home

Read this article by Beverly Beckham in which a mother describes how she felt as her children left home.

I was the sun, and the kids were my planets

I wasn't wrong about their leaving. My husband kept telling me I was. That it wasn't the end of the world when first one child, then another, and then the last packed their bags and left for college.

But it was the end of something.

I was the sun and they were the planets. And there was life on those planets, whirling, nonstop plans and parties and friends coming and going, and ideas and dreams and the phone ringing and doors slamming.

And I got to beam down on them. To watch. To glow.

And then they were gone, one after the other.

'They'll be back,' my husband said.

And he was right. They came back. But he was wrong, too, because they came back for **intervals**, not for always, not planets anymore, making their predictable orbits, but unpredictable, like shooting stars.

A chapter ends. Another chapter begins. One door closes and another door opens. The best thing a parent can give their child is wings.

But children are not birds. Parents don't let them go and build another nest and have all new offspring next year.

Saying goodbye to your children and their childhood is much harder than all the **pithy** sayings make it seem. Because that's what going to college is. It's goodbye.

It's not a death. And it's not a tragedy.

But it's not nothing, either.

The drive home alone without them is the worst. And the first few days. But then it gets better. The kids call, come home, bring their friends, and fill the house with their energy again.

Life does go on.

But I miss them, still, all these years later, the children they were, at the dinner table, beside me on the couch, talking on the phone, sleeping in their rooms, safe, home, mine.

intervals: short periods of time

pithy: short and meaningful

1   In pairs, discuss your reactions to her account. What impact does it have on you? Consider:

- how the writer describes her relationship with her children when they lived at home

- how she feels when they return to visit

- what she felt were the worst parts of the experience

- how she feels *all these years later*.

2   The writer uses four metaphors in this text. The first uses planet references. The second and third are brief references to books and doors. The final metaphor compares children to birds. Explain what each of these metaphors reveals about the mother's feelings towards her children.

- Why do you think you reacted the way you did to this article?
- What influences your responses to texts?

Language focus

In formal written English, coordinating conjunctions such as 'and', 'but', 'or' and 'so' link clauses in a sentence. You may have heard that it is grammatically incorrect to start a sentence with a coordinating conjunction, yet many published writers do it. This decision is related to the voice and the effect the writer wants to convey. Consider these two examples:

- My son said goodbye to me and then he was gone.

- My son said goodbye to me. And then he was gone.

The conjunction 'and' serves the same grammatical purpose in both sentences – it links ideas – but this placement is also used for effect. The first example seems less emotional, as if the process of the son leaving is natural and follows in an unbroken sequence. The second example seems much more emotional and dramatic. Breaking the sentence creates a pause, then starting with 'And' suggests a disruption, not only to the sentence, but to the narrator's life. It also sounds closer to spoken English, as if the writer is letting us hear her personal thoughts.

3 The mother has mixed feelings – she realises that it is natural for her children to leave, but she also feels sad. These feelings are reflected in the grammatical structure of the text. The connectives 'and' and 'but' are used frequently in this text. Here is how one learner explained the effect of these connectives:

> *The writer structures the text by describing a situation, then uses 'but' to introduce a contradicting idea – it shows how she feels conflicted. She also uses 'and' to show that life goes on.*

In pairs, discuss this learner's explanation. Does it accurately explain the use and effect of these connectives? Explain why, using specific examples.

4 Readers choose and respond to texts in different ways. Their response depends on many things, including age, gender and culture, or personal preferences about topics and themes. Listen to the audio track, in which three people discuss their reactions to the article in this session. Make notes on how and why each person reacts to the situation the writer describes.

Listening tip

When speakers justify their opinions, listen carefully to whether their opinions are based on factual or emotional matters. Emotive topics often produce emotive responses.

---

5 How do you respond to the writer's description of their feelings and experiences? Write a paragraph explaining your views. You should comment on:

- what you felt as you read the text
- why you felt this way.

Summary checklist

☐ I can identify and explain implied meanings in a descriptive account.

☐ I can interpret the meanings of a range of metaphors.

☐ I can comment on the use of conjunctions and explain their effect.

☐ I can analyse my own and other people's responses to a text.

Reading tip

When thinking about why you respond to texts in a certain way, start by considering whether the situation is one you have experienced. Ask yourself if your response is based on empathy for the characters or narrator. You could also think how the use of language affects your response.

> 9.2 The end of childhood

In this session, you will:

- read a poem aloud with expression
- explore how language and structure support the meaning of a poem
- consider the ways two writers present a similar theme
- analyse how a poet presents ideas and feelings in more than one poem.

Getting started

In Session 6.6, you learnt about extended metaphors. In pairs, write a definition for this term and think of a metaphor to express children growing up.

'To a Daughter Leaving Home'

In this session, you will read two poems by the same writer, Linda Pastan. The first poem explores the same theme as you studied in Session 9.1 – how a parent feels about their child leaving home.

When I taught you
at eight to ride
a bicycle, **loping** along
beside you
as you wobbled away
on two round wheels,
my own mouth rounding
in surprise when you pulled
ahead down the curved
path of the park,
I kept waiting
for the thud
of your crash as I
sprinted to catch up,

while you grew
smaller, more breakable
with distance,
pumping, pumping
for your life, screaming
with laughter,
the hair flapping
behind you like a
handkerchief waving
goodbye.

> **loping:** moving unevenly with large strides

1   In pairs, take turns to read the poem aloud to each other. As you do, concentrate on accurately pronouncing the hard consonant sounds at the start of words. Read the poem several times, improving your expression each time.

Peer assessment

Give your partner feedback on their:

- accuracy of pronunciation
- use of pauses to match the punctuation.

2   The poet uses a family memory of her child learning to ride a bike as an extended metaphor for the child leaving home. In your pairs, discuss what this metaphor shows about family relationships and the process of growing up.

3   Just like language choices, the punctuation and structure of a poem can also support meaning. Write a paragraph commenting on how the features of the poem link to the ideas of growing up and learning to ride a bike:

- The poem is written as a continuous sentence, using lots of commas.

- The only full stop comes at the end of the poem after the word *goodbye*.

- The poem is arranged in one long stanza rather than several smaller ones.

- The lines in the poem are uneven in length.

4   Compare this poem to the article in Session 9.1. What are the similarities and differences in the way the writers explore the same theme? Make brief notes on these listed features, then write a paragraph commenting on them in both poems:

- the choice of narrator

- the feelings of both narrators

- the use of metaphors.

Speaking tip

When reading a poem aloud, read ahead and take note of where punctuation is placed. This will help you work out where to pause or emphasise parts of the poem. Watch out for the ends of lines – some lines continue to the next line without a pause.

Writing tip

When writing about similarities between two texts, you can start sentences with 'Both poems …'. Connectives such as 'however', 'but' and 'yet' are useful when pointing out differences between texts.

'Home For Thanksgiving'

Here is a second poem by Linda Pastan. It is written from a parent's perspective and is set at Thanksgiving, an American national celebration where families eat a special meal together. The narrator thinks about her children who are growing into young adults.

The gathering family
throws shadows around us,
it is the late afternoon
Of the family.

There is still enough light
to see all the way back,
but at the windows
that light is wasting away.

Soon we will be nothing
but **silhouettes**: the sons'
as harsh
as the fathers'.

Soon the daughters
will take off their aprons
as trees take off their leaves
for winter.

Let us eat quickly–
let us fill ourselves up.
The covers of the **album** are closing
behind us.

> **silhouettes:** the dark outline of a person
> **album:** a book of photographs

5   Read the poem and make notes on:

- the images the poet uses to show the physical growth of the children

- the meaning of the last two lines.

6   Here is a view of both poems:

> In both poems, the poet uses language and structure to show the deep feelings parents have for their children.

Explain what this means, using examples from both poems.
Write 150 words in which you comment on:

- the deep feelings shown in the poems

- the way language and structure is used to show these feelings.

Summary checklist

- [ ] I can read a poem aloud accurately and with expression.
- [ ] I can explain how language, punctuation and structure support the meaning of a poem.
- [ ] I can comment on the way two writers present similar themes.
- [ ] I can analyse how a poet uses language and structure to express themes and feelings in two poems.

> 9.3 The stranger

In this session, you will:

- explore the opening of an autobiography

- perform an unscripted monologue

- plan and write a script for a film trailer.

Getting started

In pairs, discuss some film trailers you have seen. What is their purpose? What features do they contain?

Taming the Tiger

This text is an extract from the **autobiography** of Tony Anthony, a world Kung Fu champion. In it, Tony gives an account of a dramatic moment from his early childhood, where his time with his parents comes abruptly to an end.

> **Key word**
>
> **autobiography:** a text in which the writer gives an account of their own life and experiences

Extract 1

I was four years old when the stranger arrived. My father let him in and showed him through to the living room. The stranger was Chinese, like my mother. I crept down to take a peek through the half-open door. They were talking in such low voices I couldn't make out what they were saying.

Being careful not to look directly at the man, I pushed quickly past him and tried to hide behind my father's legs. Mum reached out and pulled me to her. I didn't know what to do. I looked to Dad, but he just stared at the fireplace. He was blinking heavily, as though he had something stuck in his eye.

Suddenly, the stranger took me by the wrist and Mum gave me that look, the one she used when I was to be quiet. She handed the stranger a small bag and, almost before I knew it, we were outside, walking down our garden path, leaving my parents behind.

I don't remember much about the journey. When I found myself at the airport I began to tingle with a mixture of excitement and fear. This might be a fantastic adventure, but as time passed, I grew more and more fearful. Surely Mum and Dad would come soon? Little did I know, I was on a plane bound for China.

> I awoke with a start and realised we were getting off the plane. Where were we? There was a lot of chatter, but I couldn't understand any of it. It was then I realised I was far, very far, from home.
>
> Like a frightened rabbit, I scanned the scene, hoping to catch sight of my mother or father. We stopped. Before me stood a **spindly** man dressed in a silky black jacket with wide, loose sleeves and a high collar. Later, I learned this was my grandfather. At the time, there was no introduction. I was hoisted roughly onto his horse-drawn cart and, at the click of his tongue, we pulled away into the night.

spindly: very thin

1   Reread the extract and make notes on:

  • how Tony's parents react when the stranger arrives

  • how Tony feels about what is happening to him

  • what impression you have of Tony's grandfather.

2   In groups of four, you are going to perform an **unscripted** monologue. Each group member should take one of these roles:

  • Tony   • mother

  • the stranger   • father.

Now look again at the first two paragraphs and study the actions and reactions of your character. Think about what they understand about the situation. Imagine how they feel and what they remember most about the night Tony left. Imagine that you have all been asked to describe what happened and how you felt.

Take turns to perform a 30-second monologue each. Do not write down this monologue – **improvise** as you go. Try to use gesture and facial expressions to convey your character's feelings.

Key words

unscripted: without having the words written down

improvise: to create spontaneously

Speaking tip

Before improvising in drama, make sure you understand as much about the character as possible. Imagine their personality, accent and their attitudes. Think about their emotions and how they might speak.

Peer assessment

Think about how the other group members performed their monologues. Work in groups to give feedback on:

• the choice and range of gesture and facial expressions

• how well gesture and facial expressions matched with the feelings being expressed.

3 Imagine that Tony's autobiography is being made into a film, and you have been asked to write and produce a trailer for it. Look back at Session 5.6 and remind yourself of the kind of detail you need to include when explaining a scene and the type of shots you want.

Trailers also usually include a **voiceover**, where the voice of a narrator talks directly to the viewer. This voiceover is usually like a **third person** narrator, but sometimes the voiceover is delivered by a character in the story. Here is the start of a learner's script. Read through it and:

- remind yourself of how scripts are presented

- look at the balance between dialogue and description

- decide on who will deliver your voiceover.

> **The Stranger – film trailer**
>
> *Establishing shot of front door. Close-up shot of a hand wearing a black leather glove knocking on the door.*
>
> **VOICEOVER:** I never heard the knock, but it was a knock that changed my life forever.
>
> *From the stranger's perspective, we see the door open and then see the father's sad-looking face. They say no words and walk through to a dimly lit room. Cut to close-up of Tony's eyes peering through a crack in the door. We then see it from Tony's point of view – a mysterious stranger and his mother talking very quietly.*
>
> **VOICEOVER:** I didn't know what was happening. My parents said nothing. And then the stranger took my wrist.

Start planning your script. You should:

- look again and list the main actions in the account, and also the small details

- decide which bits of the story to include

- decide if you want to use a voiceover.

Once you finished planning, write your script. Aim for 150 words.

Key words

voiceover: words spoken by a narrator to a viewer over the top of a film

third person: written from an observer's point of view using pronouns such as 'he', 'she' and 'they'

Writing tip

Trailer scripts use minimal but essential dialogue. One way to start drafting is to work out the bits of dialogue you will include. The other details about scenes and camera shots can fit around this dialogue.

❯ 9.4 A new beginning

In this session, you will:

- identify and analyse implicit meanings in a text

- consider how a reader's personal context may affect their interpretation of a text

- explore how the grammatical structure of sentences can be changed for effect.

Getting started

Some stories feature characters whose lives change very quickly and they find themselves in new and sometimes unusual situations. In pairs, note down examples of these types of stories. Did they end happily or not?

Here is another extract from *Taming the Tiger*. Tony is living in China with his grandfather, who he has been told to call 'Lowsi', which means 'master' or 'teacher'.

Extract 2

Each day began very early, around 4 or 5 o'clock. Each morning I followed Lowsi out to the courtyard where he began his morning exercises.

At first, I could only watch as Lowsi performed his strange movements. He made me stand very still and breathe deeply, in through my nose and out through my mouth. It was **tedious**.

tedious: dull and uninteresting

As the weeks went by, and I began to pick up his language, he explained that his moves were 'Tai Chi'.

I quickly gathered that my grandfather was a Grand Master in the ancient **martial art**. He was **revered** by everyone in the village.

My grandfather originated from northern China. He was born into the Soo family, a direct descendant of Gong Soo who escaped the destruction of the original Shaolin temple in 1768. Gong Soo went into hiding and continued to practise Kung Fu. His knowledge passed down from generation to generation until my grandfather, Cheung Ling Soo.

As a Shaolin monk, my grandfather was proud of this 500-year-long **heritage**. Leaving the temple of his training, he began to develop his own styles and teach the ways of Kung Fu. He soon became a Grand Master. Having no son of his own, I was his most unexpected and unlikely **disciple**. Perhaps it was for this reason that he would drive me to the harshest extremes of training. In the years ahead, Lowsi would reveal to me the secrets and treasures of the ancient art. I would become a highly disciplined disciple and an unbeatable combat warrior.

martial art: a sport such as Judo or Karate

revered: highly respected and admired

heritage: history, family background

disciple: a follower or pupil

1   Sometimes Tony discusses his feelings about his experiences explicitly, but many of his feelings are implied. Write a paragraph commenting on what Tony implies about his experience with Lowsi and what effect this has on the reader. Consider:

   •   Lowsi's actions and history

   •   what happens to Tony in the years after he is taken to China

   •   the relationship between Tony and Lowsi.

2   The context in which you read a text (for example, your age, background, and personal experiences and beliefs) can influence how you interpret and react to a text. Here are three readers' responses to *Taming the Tiger*.

Huang, 70-year-old grandfather

As an older Chinese person, I think Tony's experiences show that young people can learn a lot from some older traditions. It shows that when children listen to and learn from experts, they succeed. I liked how Lowsi is admired and that he passes on his skills to Tony. To me, the account shows the importance of family and tradition.

Kim, 22-year-old sportswoman

I enjoyed this. As a sprinter, it reminded me how difficult it is to train if you want to be a success. Even though I live in Canada and do a different sport to Tony, the account showed how hard it is to succeed in sport, and why you need somebody like Lowsi to encourage you.

Andre, 13-year-old French student

As a young person who is optimistic about life, I think Tony's story shows that although some things in life come to an end, there's always a new beginning. His account shows that change is a positive thing, and that endings can lead to a new adventure. I live in a family that believes you can achieve anything you want to if you work hard enough.

In pairs:

a   Discuss these three responses and consider how each person's age, beliefs, experiences and culture affects their interpretation of *Taming the Tiger*.

Start by identifying what you learn about each person and their overall response to the account. These are quite complex ideas so choose and adapt your language carefully to express your thoughts clearly.

b   Discuss your own response to *Taming the Tiger*. What does it mean to *you*, and how do your own beliefs and background influence this?

- How difficult was it to identify how your own beliefs and background affect the way you reacted to *Taming the Tiger*?
- How might this awareness help you when you read other texts?

Language focus

Present participle verb forms are useful ways of showing ongoing action. Present participles:

- consist of the base verb plus '–ing', such as 'holding', 'looking' and 'asking'
- are found in continuous verb forms – for example, 'I am practising', 'I was stretching'.

They are often used at the start of sentences to show two actions that are happening at the same time – for example, 'Yawning, I went to the garden to practise Tai Chi'. This emphasises the first action in the sentence. Look at these three sentences, which show the verb in different places and forms:

- I entered the cold courtyard and asked myself why I had to do these exercises.
- As I entered the cold courtyard, I asked myself why I had to do these exercises.
- Entering the cold courtyard, I asked myself why I had to do these exercises.

Continued

In the first two examples, the two actions (entering the courtyard and asking the question) are separate and distinct from each other. The third example is similar, but the present participle at the start of the sentence emphasises the continuous action and makes it feel more immediate to the reader.

3   Writers structure their sentences with particular clauses at the start in order to emphasise key information. For example, in this extract the writer uses adverbs of time (*Each day*) and prepositional phrases (*As a Shaolin monk*) to focus on important points. In both extracts, the writer also uses present participles to make the events he describes feel more real and immediate to the reader.

Look at these three examples. Rewrite each one, placing the main clause first and adding words as necessary. Which version of the sentence do you prefer and why?

a   *Being careful not to look directly at the man, I pushed quickly past him and tried to hide behind my father's legs.*

b   *Leaving the temple of his training, he began to develop his own styles and teach the ways of Kung Fu.*

c   *Having no son of his own, I was his most unexpected and unlikely disciple.*

4   Write an extra paragraph to go at the end of Extract 2.
Write in Tony's voice. Using your imagination, describe:

- continuing your exercises in the courtyard

- what you think of your grandfather.

Write 150 words and include two sentences that begin with present participle verbs.

Writing tip

When constructing a sentence starting with a present participle, start by imagining two actions you might do at the same time. Then decide which verb + '-ing' would work best at the start of the sentence.

Summary checklist

☐   I can identify meanings in a text and analyse their effect.

☐   I can explain how personal context may affect a reader's interpretation of a text.

☐   I can use present participles for effect at the start of sentences.

› 9.5 How stories end

In this session, you will:

- discuss the kind of endings you prefer in books

- consider the moral message of a story

- explore the effect of events that happen towards the end of a story

- make a judgement about a character.

Getting started

In Unit 1, you read part of the novel *When the Mountains Roared*. In pairs, discuss what you can remember about the characters and plot. Check your answers by skim reading the four extracts in Session 1.1 and 1.2.

1   Endings are an essential part of story structure. In stories with happy endings, the 'good' characters succeed and their problems are resolved. In stories with sad endings, characters are disappointed and sometimes even die. Most readers like to make predictions about how a book will end. In pairs, discuss:

- whether you like predictable endings or whether you prefer surprise endings
- whether you prefer happy or sad endings and why.

When the Mountains Roared

Now read this extract from the final chapter of *When the Mountains Roared* by Jess Butterworth. Remember that the story is narrated by Ruby. She lives with her father and grandmother, and looks after various animals, including Joey the baby kangaroo and Polly, a leopard. Prior to this extract, the two villains – Toad and Stinger – have made it seem as if Ruby's father is guilty of poaching (hunting animals illegally). Fortunately, Ruby has taken photographs proving Toad and Stinger are guilty, and she has given this evidence to the police. In the extract below, Stinger and Toad are about to be arrested.

Extract 1

Stinger nods. 'I'm tired. I've had enough of this all. I used to protect animals like this one here.' He points at me. 'Not poach them.'

'Do you know how long it's taken me to keep people away?' Toad says.

The police step towards him.

'Well I'm not going down alone,' Toad yells and he makes a sudden lunge for Joey.

Kangaroos can't hop backwards and Joey trips as she turns to get out of the way. Toad grabs her.

'No!' I shout, charging at him.

It's too late. His arms are wrapped around Joey's neck.

He's strangling her.

Dad dives at him and grabs Toad's arms, forcing them apart.

Joey wriggles out of his grip but Toad seizes her leg again.

The police tackle Toad. Joey is there, under a tangle of arms and bodies. I edge closer, trying to spot a way to get Joey free. Kangaroos scare easily. They pause a second.

'Let her go,' I say.

Polly comes leaping out of nowhere. She must have heard me cry. She snarls, leaps up and bites Toad's arm.

'Argh!' he says, letting go and grabbing his arm.

Everyone falls back.

Joey lies on the ground, panting. Her little chest rises and falls too quickly.

I rip my jumper off, cover her eyes, scoop her up, and hold her to my chest.

I turn to Stinger and Toad. 'The world isn't yours to take without thinking about others,' I say. 'You can't just hurt living things to get what you want. I know that. And I'm twelve.'

I watch from the window as Toad and Stinger are marched off the mountain.

The police officer opens my bedroom door. 'Knock, knock,' she says. 'Is the animal going to be all right?'

Joey doesn't come out for the rest of the day. I keep checking on her to make sure she's still breathing. I don't let Polly come in and see me, even when she paws at the door, in case Joey feels scared.

2   In this part of the story, the villains are captured and Toad
    is bitten. In pairs, discuss:

    •   what moral message the writer suggests by the arrest of the
         villains – how do you react to this event?

    •   why the writer might have included the villain being bitten by
         an animal?

3   Towards the end of most stories, all the major problems are
    resolved. Here, the arrest of the villains clears up the most
    important problem, but a further dramatic event takes place – the
    kangaroo Joey is injured. This is a much more personal issue for
    Ruby, rather than the more public problem caused by the villains.

    In pairs, discuss why the writer might have introduced this new
    problem at this point. What does it show about Ruby and what
    effect does it have on the reader?

4 Which of these statements do you think accurately describes Ruby and her situation at this point in the story? Write a sentence for each statement explaining why you agree or disagree with it. Use quotations to support your points.

a Stinger realises that Ruby's attitude towards animals is the right one.

b Ruby's biggest concern is making sure Toad is arrested.

c Ruby is brave and manages to rescue Joey on her own.

d Ruby is the only person who seems concerned about Joey.

e Although Ruby is the youngest character, she is the wisest.

f The writer expects the reader to agree with Ruby's views.

5 Write a paragraph explaining how Ruby is presented in this extract. Think about your work on heroes in Unit 5 – would you describe Ruby as a hero? Explain your view using evidence from the extract.

Reading tip

When making a judgement about a character, think carefully about the criteria you judge them against. For example, if you are asked to judge whether a character is a hero, start by writing a list of heroic qualities, then evaluate the character against these qualities.

Self-assessment

Reread your paragraph about Ruby.

- How thoroughly have you given your view of Ruby – is it convincing?

- How well have you selected evidence from the extract – are your quotations the most useful ones to support the view? Why or why not?

Summary checklist

☐ I can explain the different types of story endings and express a preference.

☐ I can comment on the moral message of a story.

☐ I can explain how events near the conclusion of a story impact the reader.

☐ I can express an opinion about a character's presentation at the end of a story.

〉 9.6 Learning things

Getting started

Some texts end with the central character feeling that they have developed or learnt something about themselves. In pairs, discuss stories where characters have noticeably changed by the end. In what ways do these characters change and how does it affect your interpretation of the story?

Key word

epilogue: a section at the end of a story that acts as a conclusion to what has happened

You are going to read the rest of the final chapter of *When the Mountains Roared*. Before the whole story begins, Ruby's mother had died. The book ends with an **epilogue**, showing what happens a little later.

Extract 2

Later, Grandma brings me fresh **papaya** cut into slices. 'Why don't you go outside and get some fresh air?' she says, as I nibble on the fruit. 'I'll look after Joey for a bit.'

'Okay,' I say **listlessly** and amble outside.

I sit on the wall and hug my knees, listening to the breeze rustle through the pine trees and watching the butterflies.

Footsteps approach behind me.

'Can I join you?' asks Dad.

I nod.

Dad sits next to me on the wall.

I shift my position and swing my legs over the side.

'You know, I see your mum in everything around us,' he says.

'You don't talk about her much any more,' I say, my voice wavering slightly. 'It makes me feel like we're forgetting her.'

'Your mum lives on in you, Ruby. She would be so very proud of what you did today and how you saved the cub.'

I smile. I know he's right. I can feel it in my bones.

That night, I realise I'm not afraid any more.

I'm not scared of the dark, or of falling asleep. Going through everything I did to save the leopard made me realise I can handle more than I thought. I roll over and I fall asleep clutching my necklace, and dream of Mum.

Epilogue

Two weeks later, Praveen and I are lying on rugs on the veranda outside, next to the orange lilies. It's the middle of the monsoon and we're surrounded by a cloud that drifts inside if we leave a window open.

'Ruby?' calls Grandma.

She bustles through the door carrying Joey, who leaps out of her arms and into mine.

'She left the pouch for the first time by herself!'

I hug Joey, stopping myself from squeezing her too tightly.

'I knew you'd recover,' I whisper to her. 'You're tougher than you look.'

Just like me.

papaya: a tropical fruit

listlessly: without any energy or enthusiasm

1   Imagine you have been asked to give a brief speech to younger learners in your school about *When the Mountains Roared,* particularly the ending of the story. You have to summarise the characters, the main problem and what happens at the end.

Start by collating the information about the book from Sessions 1.1, 1.2, 9.5 and 9.6. Next, consider your audience – remember that you are speaking to younger learners so adapt your language to suit your audience. Decide the degree of formality you will use and how you will use gesture and visual aids as you talk. Your talk should last one minute. Write it, then ask a partner to listen to it and give you some feedback.

Writing tip

When writing a speech for a specific audience, approach things from their point of view. Think about their knowledge of the topic, what key things they need to know and their understanding of spoken English.

As you draft your speech, think about how it will sound from your audience's point of view.

Peer assessment

Listen to your partner's speech, trying to imagine you are a younger learner.

Give your partner some feedback on:

- how clear their use of language was
- any parts which might need redrafting.

2   Now imagine you have to give a speech to an older audience – a teacher who is considering reading *When the Mountains Roared* with their class next year. Your task is to:

- briefly explain the characters, basic plot and how the book ends
- persuade the teacher to put this book on the school's reading list.

Remember that teachers often select books for their classes that have positive moral messages, so you may want to use this in your speech. You will also need to adapt your language for your audience. Decide on the degree of formality, and how you will use gestures and visual aids. Start by planning reasons why classes might enjoy this book. Present your speech to your teacher – it should last one minute.

3   In pairs, discuss the different ways you used language in your speeches. What impact do you think these variations might have had on your audience?

4   Themes emerge clearly at the end of a story. One theme in *When the Mountains Roared* is the importance of family. It shows how families care for each other, and how family members who have died live on through their children. In pairs:

- find examples from the text that show the importance of family

- discuss other stories where this theme is also explored.

5   Another theme in this story is the importance of standing up for what you believe in and doing the right thing. Ruby believes that humans should protect animals. Write a short story about a character who stands up for what they believe in.

Use all the knowledge you have gained in this book to plan, structure and write your story. As you draft your work, reflect and self-assess as you go. Your finished work should be about 250 words.

Summary checklist

☐ I can summarise a story and describe it for a young audience.
☐ I can plan, write and deliver a persuasive speech about a story for an older audience.
☐ I can explain how themes are presented at the end of a story.
☐ I can plan and write a story with a given theme.

Check your progress

Answer these questions.

1. Explain the different possible effects of starting a sentence with a coordinating conjunction.

2. 'The punctuation and structure of a poem can support meaning'. Explain what this means with examples.

3. Give some tips for performing an improvised monologue.

4. What is a present participle? Write a sentence beginning with a present participle verb.

5. Explain the two different ways stories end. Give some examples.

6. Give an account of the choices you need to make when speaking to different audiences.

Project

In groups of four, you are going to give a presentation on story endings. Try to show the patterns and typical ways in which stories end, and whether books belonging to different genres end in different ways.

Start by choosing four books – one for each group member. Each group member must select a different genre or type of story – something they have read and are familiar with.

Then, individually reread the ending of your chosen book. Make notes on:

- the genre
- what challenges the central character faced
- if (and how) these were overcome
- how the central character developed or what they learnt
- what themes or ideas emerged at the end
- whether the book has a happy or sad ending.

After making notes, plan your presentation as a group. Explore any patterns in the ways the stories end and summarise your main findings as a group.

Next, work out the best way to present your findings. Each group member should describe their book's ending, speaking for at least two minutes about it. Remember to summarise the overall patterns – the similarities and differences between books. Consider if visual aids might help and decide who will speak at which point.

› Glossary

genre	a particular type of text – for example, adventure, comedy, crime, science fiction	61
gesture	movements of the hands or arms to add emphasis or bring a story to life	15
gist	the main point of a text	28
glossary	an alphabetical list of words or phrases from a text, with their meanings	35
humour	when things are funny, or things that are comical	103
hyperbole	exaggerated statements	66
imperative	a word or phrase styled as an order or command	100
implicit information	ideas and details that readers have to work out for themselves from the text	51
improvise	to create spontaneously	234
informal language	a more relaxed form of English, used when speaking or in more casual written texts, such as emails to friends	30
interior shot	an image showing the inside of a building	144
linking adverb	an adverb that shows a sequence in time or contrast (for example, 'afterwards')	211
literal	describing something in a straightforward way, using the original, direct meaning of words	40
metaphor	a type of comparison that describes one thing as if it is something else	40
mime	to act something out without words or sounds, using only body language, movement and gesture	214
minor sentence	a sentence that does not contain a main verb	31
modal verb	one of nine verbs used to show possibility – 'can', 'may', 'must', 'shall', 'will', 'could', 'might', 'should', 'would'	124
monologue	a story or speech given by one character	75
mood	the feeling created by the words, sounds and images in a text	47
morphology	the study of how words are formed and their relationship with other words	34
narrative	a series of connected events that are written or spoken	118
narrator	the person telling the story	12
non-fiction	writing that is about real events and facts	19
non-standard English	words and grammatical patterns that fall outside the conventional forms of English	67
noun phrase	a phrase that contains a noun and describes the qualities of an object	215
opinion	a personal view or judgement about something, not necessarily based on fact or knowledge	21
oxymoron	a figure of speech that combines two contradictory ideas	66
pace	the speed at which someone speaks or how quickly events take place in a story	47
passive voice	where the verb comes before the person or thing, so the verb acts upon the subject	197

personification	a type of figurative language in which an object is described as if it has human characteristics	19
perspective	the 'angle' that a story or account is told from – whose 'eyes' the reader sees it through	121
phonetic spelling	spelling words as they sound	130
plot	the main events of a story, film, novel or play in sequence from beginning to end	43
prediction	an idea about what might happen in the future	42
prefix	letters added to the beginning of a word to make a new word with a different meaning	34
preposition	a word or group of words used before a noun or pronoun to show place, direction, time, etc. (for example, 'above', 'below', 'under', 'in')	215
prepositional phrase	a group of words consisting of a preposition followed by a noun (or sometimes an adverb or another preposition)	215
pronoun	a word that stands in for a noun to avoid repetition; pronouns can be subject personal pronouns (e.g. 'I', 'you'), object personal pronouns (e.g. 'him', 'them') or possessive pronouns (e.g. 'mine', 'ours')	39
prose	the form of language found in novels and non-fiction texts such as articles, written in paragraphs rather than verse	13
reporting verb	a verb that conveys the action of speaking – used with both direct and reported speech	48
rhetorical questions	questions designed to make a point rather than expecting an answer	100
rhyme	words where the end part sounds the same (for example, 'feet' rhymes with 'meat')	164
rhythm	a regular, repeating pattern of sound or 'beat', common in music and poetry	164
root word	the basic form of a word that other words with related meanings are based on	34
scan	to look through a text quickly to find particular details	56
script	the words and actions from a play written down for the actors to use	13
secondary character	a supporting character in a story; not the main character	160
sequence	the order of events in a story	35
setting	the location where a story takes place	39
simile	a type of figurative language in which one thing is compared to something else using the words 'as' or 'like'	19
simple sentence	a sentence with one main clause	30
skim	read a text quickly to get the overall idea	28
stage directions	words in a script that explain what is happening on stage or tell the actors how to move and speak	15
standard English	the most widely accepted form of English that is not specific to a particular region	27
stanza	a group of lines of poetry, forming a unit	208
stereotype	a familiar but simplified character type	67

> Acknowledgements

The author and publisher acknowledge the following sources of copyright material and are grateful for the permissions granted. While every effort has been made, it has not always been possible to identify the sources of all the material used, or to trace all copyright holders. If any omissions are brought to our notice, we will be happy to include the appropriate acknowledgements on reprinting.

Unit 1 Abridged extracts from *When the Mountains Roared* by Jess Butterworth, reproduced by permission of Orion Children's Books, an imprint of Hachette Children's Books, Carmelite House, 50 Victoria Embankment, London imprint, EC4Y 0DZ (extracts from this source also appear in Unit 9); 'Loneliness', 'Visitors' and 'Written on the Wall at Chang's Hermitage' by Kenneth Rexroth, from the original by Tu Fu, from *ONE HUNDRED POEMS FROM THE CHINESE*, copyright ©1971 by Kenneth Rexroth. Reprinted by permission of New Directions Publishing Corp.; Adapted from article 'Tsunami witness: I saw the sea start to rise. There was terror and anguish' by Jocelyn Tordecilla Jorquera, reproduced with the permission of Guardian News & Media Ltd 2020; **Unit 2** Adapted text and illustrations from *Grandmother's Song*, used by permission of Barefoot Books, Inc. Text copyright © 1998 by Barbara Soros. Illustrations copyright © 1998 by Jackie Morris. The moral rights of Barbara Soros and Jackie Morris have been asserted; 'Jessie Emily Scofield' by Judy Williams - published in *Critical Quarterly*, volume 31, issue 2 (1989), reproduced with permission of the Licensor through PLSclear; **Unit 3** Abridged excerpts from *THE LOST ISLAND OF TAMARIND* by Nadia Aguiar. Copyright © 2008 by Nadia Aguiar. Reprinted by permission of Feiwel and Friends. All Rights Reserved; **Unit 4** Abridged excerpts from *THE MAZE RUNNER (MAZE RUNNER, BOOK ONE): BOOK ONE* by James Dashner, copyright © 2009 by James Dashner. Used by permission of Chicken House Publishers and Delacorte Press, an imprint of Random House Children's Books, a division of Penguin Random House LLC. All rights reserved; **Unit 5** Abridged extract from *Tokyo* by Graham Marks published by Bloomsbury, reproduced with the permission of Bloomsbury Publishing Plc; Abridged from article 'Life as a young carer' by Kate Hilpern, reproduced with the permission of Guardian News & Media Ltd 2020; Abridged from article 'Supporting young careers' by Liz Burton, reproduced with the permission of High Speed Training Limited; Abridged from article 'Stan Lee's final creation was a Chinese superhero' by Zheping Huang and Viola Zhou, reproduced with the permission of South China Morning Post; Abridged from article 'When Stan Lee created an Indian superhero to keep Mumbai safe' by Maria Thomas, reproduced with the permission of CCC on behalf of Quartz India; **Unit 6** Abridged from article 'How Monsters Under the Bed Became a Common Childhood Fear' by Joshua A. Krisch, reproduced with the permission of Fatherly; 'The Scorpion' by Hillaire Belloc; Abridged from article 'Monster fatbergs' by Chris Baynes © Chris Baynes/The Independent News; **Unit 7** 'The Plantation' © 2021 by Ovo Adagha, abridged and reproduced with the permission of author; **Unit 8** Abridged from article 'Top 10 Ways to Make Better Decisions' by Kate Douglas and Dan Jones, New Scientist, May 2007, reproduced with the permission of Tribute Content Agency; Abridged from article 'Tourist feared he would die clinging to outback train' by Bonnie Malkin in Sydney for the Daily Telegraph, 9th June 2009 ©

Bonnie Malkin/Telegraph Media Group Limited 2009; Abridged from article 'To be a refugee is to make impossible choices' by Elizabeth Olson, Reprinted with permission from Oxfam America; Abridged from article 'Do developed countries have a responsibility to welcome refugees? Yes' by Norashikin Mohamad from iThink Magazine, issue 23, ilovereading.sg; **Unit 9** Abridged from article 'I was the sun, and the kids were my planets' by Beverly Beckham. Originally published in the Boston Globe, August 2006, reproduced with the permission of Beverly Beckham; 'To a Daughter Leaving Home' from *Carnival Evening: New and Selected Poems 1968-1998* (W.W. Norton & Company) and 'Home for Thanksgiving' from Setting the Table (Dryad Press) by Linda Pastan ©1980, 1998 by Linda Pastan. Used by permission of Linda Pastan in care of the Jean V. Naggar Literary Agency, Inc and W.W. Norton & Company Inc.; Abridged extract from *Taming the Tiger* by Tony Anthony & Angela Little, copyright © Authentic Media 2004, reproduced with the permission of Great Commission Society.

Thanks to the following for permission to reproduce images:

Cover image created by Justin Rowe; Inside Unit 1 Westend61/GI; Abinav Manikantan/GI; ilbusca/GI; Benjawan Sittidech/GI; Jong-Won Heo/GI; Rudi Hulshof/GI; Aaron Von Hagen/GI; Aumphotography/GI; George Balyasov/GI; Ed Freeman/GI; Anton Petrus/GI; Delta Images/GI; Yew! Images/GI; RelaxFoto.de/GI; Unit 2 IlexImage/GI; Juan Carlos Vindas/GI; Alvis Upitis/GI; kikikentucky/GI; Enrique Aguirre Aves/GI; Todd Leckie/GI; Ippei Naoi/GI; Rike/GI; ilbusca/GI; Sangkhom Hungkhunthod/GI; TJ Drysdale/GI; Unit 3 Westend61/GI; Granger/Shutterstock; Everett Collection Inc/Alamy Stock Photo; JordeAngjelovik/GI; YS graphic/GI; OktalStudio/GI; R.Tsubin/GI; Gunnar Örn Árnason/GI; Marc Guitard/GI; PamelaJoeMcFarlane/GI; Kehao Chen/GI; Nick Venton/GI; Stockbyte/GI; GettyImages/GI; sarote pruksachat/GI; simonlong/GI; Unit 4 MR.Cole_Photographer/GI; Vince Streano/GI; Busakorn Pongparnit/GI; NurPhoto/GI; Marco_Piunti/GI; Tom Odulate/GI; Klaus Vedfelt/GI; Dina Belenko Photography/GI; gremlin/GI; Westend61/GI; gremlin/GI; M. McQ./GI; LANDMARK MEDIA/Alamy Stock Photo; IndiaPicture/GI; Busà Photography/GI; Cavan Images/GI; John Lund/GI; Unit 5 Luis Alvarez/GI; Stephen F. Somerstein/GI; Paul Bradbury/GI; Colin Anderson Productions pty ltd/GI; Koukichi Takahashi/GI; PictureNet/GI; recep-bg/GI; Spyridon Evangelatos/GI; Halfpoint Images/GI; SDI Productions/GI; SolStock/GI; kirkchai benjarusameeros/GI; yogysic/GI; SOPA Images/GI; Amanda Edwards/GI; Darryl Estrine/GI; guruXOOX/GI; Unit 6 Alexlky/GI; Bastetamn/GI; PeopleImages/GI; Donald Iain Smith/GI; Alex Ortega/GI; Lindsay Berger/GI; Trudie Davidson/GI; Gregoria Gregoriou Crowe/GI; Mark Newman/GI; gawrav/GI; ADRIAN DENNIS/GI; Martin Schroeder/GI; Wing To Yim/GI; WIN-Initiative/GI; Unit 7 ISSOUF SANOGO/GI; peeterv/GI; William Andrew/GI; Mohammed Husain/GI; Jorge Fernández/GI; Timothy Allen/GI; STEFAN HEUNIS/AFP via Getty Images; Timothy Allen/GI; Marianne Purdie/GI; Jasmin Merdan/GI; iom/GI; Alexandre Morin-Laprise/GI; Ishii Koji/GI; Unit 8 AscentXmedia/GI; John Cumming/GI; selimaksan/GI; PM Images/GI; Christina Reichl Photography/GI; PM Images/GI; LOUISA GOULIAMAKI/GI; ARIS MESSINIS/GI; Stocktrek Images/GI; Mario Gutiérrez./GI; georgeclerk/GI; Unit 9 Tetra Images/GI; Ariel Skelley/GI; SDI Productions/GI; Ash Lindsey Photography/GI; Image Source/GI; Yaorusheng/GI; Rubberball/Mike Kemp/GI; somethingway/GI; photosindia/GI; Photographed by Photost0ry/GI; gawrav/GI; Terry Wong/GI; Image Source/GI

GI = Getty Images